MANUSCRIPT ACCIDENTALS: FICTA IN FOCUS 1350-1450

MUSICOLOGICAL STUDIES & DOCUMENTS

ARMEN CARAPETYAN
Director

MANUSCRIPT ACCIDENTALS: FICTA IN FOCUS 1350-1450

by

ANDREW HUGHES

MUSICOLOGICAL STUDIES & DOCUMENTS

27

ANDREW HUGHES

MANUSCRIPT ACCIDENTALS: FICTA IN FOCUS 1350-1450

AMERICAN INSTITUTE OF MUSICOLOGY

1972

CONTENTS

TABLES

PREFACE

If an "occupational disease of system-building... is a compulsion to push the logic of the system to extremes"* then in pursuing the theory of chromaticism in the Middle Ages I have probably pushed farther than necessary for most purposes. Indeed it may be doubted whether the system is consistent enough to be thus extended: certainly theorists of the time met with difficulty. Nevertheless, the many impasses and conflicts noted by modern authorities in handling medieval chromaticism suggest that our view of the topic may be too narrow, a condition perhaps resulting from our search for definitive, consistent and immutable meanings. We rigidly define an accidental. That the medieval theorist defined it differently should have warned us that our own interpretation would not suffice.

Pushing towards the horizon tended to illuminate more clearly the middle ground and enabled me to offer new suggestions for some features hitherto inexplicable or controversial. Clarification in these areas has inevitably raised other difficulties which remain in the distant shadows, where the logic of the system tends to become obscure. But we can proceed only step by step.

If I have explored any new territory it is because others have dared to tread the foreground. My greatest debt is probably to Dr Margaret Bent, who first emphasised the crucial difference between musica recta and musica ficta, as well as the position of B♭ in, and the theoretical preference for, the former. These discoveries surveyed the middle ground, and my own work is largely mapping in more detail. The valuable contributions of earlier authorities, whose investigation of numerous topics represented the most difficult and dangerous steps towards a solution, had, I believe, reached a barrier beyond which we seemed unable to progress.

This may have been because of their attempts to relate ficta to modal theory, in which a scale may have either B♮ or B♭ but not both, equally and without discrimination. In our joint examination of chromaticism, Mrs Bent and I did not find it necessary even to refer to modes: I take it therefore that they are irrelevant.

Mrs Bent and I had intended to publish our work together, under the title *Musica Recta, Musica Ficta and the Old Hall Manuscript*†. Even-

* Dwight Mcdonald, in "McLuhan, Pro and Con", ed. R. Rosenthal, Pelican, 1969, p.34.

† As announced in *Early English Church Music* 8, London 1968, p.xiv, n.1 and in *Musica Disciplina* XXIII, 1969, p.22, n.12.

tually, discovering our respective contributions differed considerably in style and method of presentation, and exhausted by three thousand pages of trans-Atlantic collaboration* for the new edition of Old Hall, we reluctantly decided to continue separately. The amount by which the following study depends on Mrs Bent's work is incalculable.

If I were to make the claim that "adding accidentals no longer represents a major problem of editing..." it would have to be qualified with "...music of the period about 1400": for me the chromatic difficulties of music from any later era remain as great. To claim there are no problems would not be true; to claim solutions would be foolhardy; to explain clearly theories of this abstruse topic is taxing. At most I hope to have indicated that theoretically the field is much more complex than has previously been made obvious, and to have suggested some ideas to be pursued later. The detailed editorial procedures given at the end are the joint work of Mrs Bent and myself and represent an attempt to limit the theoretical complexities in favour of practical methods.

I believe it necessary to repeat here the sentiments with which I end Appendix II. Many aspects still need to be studied, and much more statistical evidence is required. We must heed Lowinsky's warning about drawing wide conclusions from narrow evidence. But the publicising of ideas and interesting relationships from a few sources can indicate what we should search for in a wider repertory. In that search, however, we must beware of noting *only* those features which tend to confirm conclusions only tentatively expressed. This study, although it uses what facts are available, is about ideas.

Professor Gaston Allaire, of the Université de Moncton, is about to publish, in this same series, a book entitled "The Theory of the Hexachords and Solmization and the Modal System". I was not able to consult this study in detail, but the author very kindly sent me his chapter and section headings: the topics of ficta and solmization are evidently closely related and there are a few parts of Allaire's work which are clearly in common with my own. One such area is the matter of conflicting signatures, which Allaire refers to, without the implicit assumption of conflict, as Contrasting Signatures. But his general purpose, that of elucidating the relation between modes and solmization and the rules for the latter, is quite different from mine, which is to show how written-in accidentals can throw light on extemporised chromaticism.

I wish to thank Professor Allaire for his willingness to share

* Including letters, notes, music manuscript and typescript, and proof-pages of the edition itself.

his ideas before publication. My thanks are also due to Mrs Bent for her frequent advice throughout the formulation of my part of our joint work. For proof reading, typing and much other assistance I should like to thank my wife and my mother. Naturally, the mistakes are my own.

Andrew Hughes
University of Toronto
Christmas 1969.

TERMINOLOGY AND SYMBOLS

Pitches: where it is not important to identify the octave, pitches are given in capital letters; otherwise the medieval system proceeding Γ A...a...$\overset{a}{a}$... is used.

Syllables: occasionally, to save space in Tables, ut re mi fa sol la are abbreviated to their initial letters.

Examples: these are identified by number and folio in the Old Hall MS, followed by the stave number in small Roman numerals, where necessary. A textual tag is normally included. The location in the new edition is also noted, but because of the requirements of modern transcription the musical details occasionally differ.

Accidentals: where the syllable mi is specified, ♮-♯ is shown, since the two symbols are usually indistinguishable. Otherwise ♮ and ♯ have their usual meaning.

Transposition: unless otherwise qualified, transposition always means by fourth or fifth, up or down according to context. Thus, "twice-transposed" refers to the pitch two fifths (i.e., a tone) distant.

Degree: the degree of an accidental always refers to its position in the standard circle of fifths. Thus, A♭ is a third degree flat, C♯ a second degree sharp. Farther or nearer refer to the distance of an accidental from the beginning of the circle.

Section numbers and Index: to avoid an additional proof stage, and to simplify cross references, the text is divided into sections numbered consecutively throughout. Numbers in parentheses, and those in the Index, refer to these sections. Note that sections 11, 12, and 13, dealing with Ugolino's chapter on Musica Ficta, are subdivided by the sentence numbers of the original Latin.

Footnotes: items listed in the Bibliography are referred to by short titles in footnotes.

INTRODUCTION

1. Performing copies from the Middle Ages rarely seem to be marked with the complete range of accidentals needed to make the music conform with what the theorists say about musica ficta. The idea that the treatises were referring only to a speculative technique of no relevance to performance must be rejected because, quite plainly, even apart from the requirements of theorists, the manuscripts themselves rarely have all the accidentals needed for a satisfactory result. Extra chromaticism must usually be added. The problem of *what* and *where* accidentals must be added has received much attention in the items listed in the bibliography, but some related problems have not been studied. It is surely of importance to know, or at least to ask, *when* accidentals were added: at performance, extempore — before the first reading of a piece, so that the score for rehearsals is the final one — at the first reading, extempore, but with adjustments at later rehearsals?

2. Related to this question is one which asks *who* was responsible: the performers, independently — or in collaboration — or some other agent such as the precentor? In this respect we must consider the style of the music and ask whether extempore addition by the performer (the solution favoured nowadays) would be practical: if the individual parts are clearly for soloists such a procedure may be feasible, but it is hardly so for complex choral polyphony. Unless controlled by absolutely strict rules, which in a sense negate the practice, extemporisation is possible only with a single performer to a part.

A third question concerns *how* accidentals were added. Having discovered what accidentals to add and where to add them, how did the performers maintain them through rehearsals and performance?

For us, searching for definitive, consistent solutions, the answers would be obvious: the precentor marks every copy as necessary before the first rehearsal. This is the modern editor's function when dealing with early music, and we have to recognise clearly that it represents the imposition of a contemporary attitude onto an art in which consistency mattered little. Had this been the medieval method, surely one fully 'corrected' performance edition would have been preserved? No single answer can exist. But we can reasonably eliminate some of the possibilities.

3. 'Correction' of the score before first rehearsal, allowing the precentor to act individually, or as a spokesman for the performers in collaboration, would produce a final version of the music. We cannot entirely reject this approach, so long as we see that extra accidentals are kept through rehearsals and performance by some means which does not require them to be noted fully in the manuscripts. There is no evidence that performers used fully marked copies and the failure to enter complete chromaticism in any manuscript forces us to the conclusion that performers must have relied on their memories. This need not surprise us. The character of the Middle Ages as a predominantly oral culture, not relying heavily on visual aids, should hardly need arguing, and the training of the musician particularly emphasised reliance on the memory. Medieval singers were subjected to disciplines which must have equipped them for life with enviable musical memories[1] and the whole basis of solmization rested on the ability to hear wrong syllables rather than to see wrong notes, and to sing correct syllables rather than to see correct accidentals: *the intervals of the solmization syllables should be correctly recited so that a semitone is not sung instead of a tone*[2]. The quite reasonable assumption that medieval performers were able to remember the necessary accidentals, once they had been ascertained, allows us to dispense with the problem of maintaining the 'correct' solution.

But providing a completely correct score before rehearsal deprives the practice of any vestige of extemporisation, which the circumstances indicate as one of the basic qualities of the art. We therefore ought to reject prior chromatic correction as the sole, or even as the most likely, method of arriving at the solution, since it does not allow the performer the rights he evidently enjoyed.

4. Complete and correct extemporisation at performance or first rehearsal must also have been out of the question even for skilled soloists, because no set of rules detailed enough to cover all the situations was in existence and no-one has since been able to deduce any such principles from the available evidence. Expert performers, familiar with the harmonic vocabulary and general style, may have been able to feel the direction of the music and to make the necessary adjustments at first reading, but only with the simplest and most conventional piece of music. Some English descant of the fourteenth century may qualify for such treatment, but the probability is that these pieces were chorally sung, raising the difficulty of group extemporisation. The assumption that a first rehearsal could not, in most instances, have realised a correct version

1. F. Ll. Harrison, "Music in Medieval Britain", London 1958, pp.5-6, 18-19.
2. Coussemaker IV, 250. See also Bent, diss., 413.

of the music may be further justified, and in this additional reason lies the most obvious crux of the whole difficulty about *what* accidentals to add: in practice, chromatic alteration has to be applied for both melodic and harmonic purposes and the two are often not compatible. In polyphony, accidentals cannot be added successfully by considering only the melodic or harmonic situation independently, and at first sight the medieval singer had in front of him only the former. How can theoretical evidence, which mainly gives harmonic prescriptions, be of any help to the singer who has only the melodic part before him (or who has had only that part from which to memorise)? On the other hand, if accidentals were added as a purely extempore technique by the singer with only the melody in mind, what then were the theorists describing? In order to add accidentals by either harmonic principles or by balancing melodic against harmonic requirements, study and correction of the score as a whole before first rehearsal is necessary, a procedure we have previously discarded.

5. Rejecting these solutions leaves only one possibility, that of more or less extempore addition at a first rehearsal, causing some unacceptable harmonic results, followed by gradual adjustment at later rehearsals to eliminate direct clashes and unmusical sounds. Certainly for much medieval music several rehearsals must have been needed, to resolve problems of notation, proportions and inaccuracies. For accidentals to have been added extempore, applied by the singer to the single melodic part before him, melodic principles must have been foremost. The harmonic clashes inevitably caused by this approach would need to be adjusted at second rehearsal, and the theorists' harmonic principles are just what we need for the singers' mutual adjustments in practice. Melodic principles could be reduced to a simple set of rules, easily remembered and therefore not requiring a visual reminder in the form of a written accidental, nor any theoretical statement: the frequent exceptions to these rules caused by vertical clashes could hardly be reduced to simple formulas and would have to be memorised in their contexts, or some visual reminder would be necessary. This brings us to the subject of this study, the manuscript accidental and its function. If the medieval memory was so reliable, what purpose does the accidental serve? To suggest its use at points where memory failed is to vitiate the previous arguments about the way in which chromaticism may have been realised: moreover, the accidental is often written in at points where the need for it would in any case be obvious and the symbol itself quite unnecessary (62). Doubtless some manuscript accidentals were to reinforce weak memories, but for the majority we have to seek some other reason.

Notwithstanding the theoretical prescriptions about obligatory musica ficta, because of its very nature as an improvisatory art, because of the failure of the manuscripts to be unequivocal in noting it, and because of theorists' statements that beauty is one reason for it, extempore chromatic ornamentation must have been variable in many respects. There is no one correct method of realising a piece of music and, apart from certain limitations, the amount of chromaticism must have depended on local tastes, individual skills, musical styles, and on one's interpretation of 'beauty'. Even if there were a single overall solution, the complexities of adjusting obligatory and optional melodic and harmonic requirements must have resulted in places of ambiguity, of equal choice between two or more alternatives. Even where no ambiguity exists, it is possible that the composer himself may have had a preference, may have wished for some reason, artistic or otherwise, to break an understood rule.

6. For clarification, then, or for precise specification, the manuscript accidentals may be our only clue to the correct way of altering a passage, of limiting the numerous choices available. Manuscript accidentals should therefore be rated as primary evidence, to be thoroughly analysed before proceeding with further chromatic changes: they stand as the only clues before the performer, to guide his extemporisation. They may serve as landmarks or signposts pointing the way to a sharpward movement rather than the flatward one expected and it may be that, if extensive manuscript accidentals are present, the chromaticism of the piece is clearly defined, reducing many choices to a single one. In this respect manuscript accidentals would serve to concentrate the chromaticism of a whole passage onto a few points of ambiguity and we would do well to focus on such accidentals in detail to find out their repertory of meanings, before tackling the problem of what unwritten accidentals to add and where to add them. The purpose of this study is to treat the manuscript accidental as a focal point of chromatic alteration and to investigate its implications.

The theoretical background

7. In order to give a more complete foundation for the subsequent arguments, it will be useful to examine the theoretical statements of contemporary writers. This monograph deals with the decades around 1400: rather than reviewing the relevant passages of a number of treatises from many eras, a practice which has frequently been followed, I insert here a translation of and commentary on a single author's remarks on accidentals and musica ficta. The passage is as comprehensive as most and may serve as a representative early fifteenth century discussion of the topic: although other writers may refer to different features, these are normally abstractions from the sort of material given here, or are explanations of exactly the same underlying traits, but from the point of view of the singer rather than composer or listener, and so on[3].

From most theoretical references to musica ficta, including the important chapter by Ugolino of Orvieto, written about 1430[4], only the meaningful, information-laden passages have been published in translation. Unfortunately, even in the middle of the most repetitious and uninteresting material, which generally remains unexplored, there can occur a single illuminating phrase, such as the one referred to below (20) buried within the serpentine and rambling sentence 66 of Ugolino's chapter[5]. In places the chapter is extraordinarily long-winded and could not be translated in a parallel form and still be readable. My translation is virtually a paraphrase in which the important sentences are rendered as close to the original as possible while the remainder is condensed by means of generalisation or by telescoping or by use of such words as "former" in place of repeated phrases.

8. Because the subject matter is complex I precede the actual treatise with a review of the three topics discussed, referring where necessary to Ugolino's sentence numbers. To understand these topics the reader must be thoroughly familiar with the theoretical system of solmization and hexachords in standard use during the Middle Ages. Table I shows the gamut of pitches available to a composer without restriction and the solmization syllables applied to them, as well as the hexachords into which the syllables were organized. Theorists derived these pitches from the monochord before any others, calling the whole series musica vera or musica recta (Ugolino, 1-5, 19-26, *passim*). Later, they derived chromatic semitones between the musica recta pitches, and called this series of notes musica ficta: such 'imagined' notes were available only

3. Bent, diss., 389-429 and many of the articles listed in the Bibliography give treatment of contemporary theoretical evidence.
4. *Die Musik in Geschichte und Gegenwart:* Ugolino.
5. See also my article "Ugolino: the Monochord and Musica Ficta", in *Musica Disciplina* XXIII, 1969, pp.21-39, which deals with Ugolino's other statements on musica ficta. Little or nothing occurs in those statements which is not more fully treated in the main chapter on the topic, given here, but the two versions should be compared.

under certain conditions. That musica recta constitutes the normal series for a piece of music is clearly implied by the nomenclature — recta is correct or normal while ficta is false or fictitious — as well as by the conventional statement that *we may use it [musica ficta] only where absolutely necessary* (Ugolino, 10-12). Philippe de Vitry puts it most clearly, after mentioning falsa musica: *nothing regular ought to accept the false, but rather the true* (Coussemaker III, 18a).

TABLE I

The normal gamut, showing musica recta.

ee							LA
dd						*la*	SOL
cc						*sol*	FA
♮♮							MI
♭♭						*fa*	
aa					la	*mi*	RE
g					sol	*re*	UT
f					fa	*ut*	
e				LA	mi		
d			*la*	SOL	re		
c			*sol*	FA	ut		
♮				MI			
♭			*fa*				
a		la	*mi*	RE			
G		sol	*re*	UT			
F		fa	*ut*				
E	LA	mi					
D	SOL	re					
C	FA	ut					
♮	MI						
A	RE						
Γ	UT						

Capitals: hard hexachord
Lower case: natural hexachord
Italic: soft hexachord

The distinction between recta and ficta is not that of white notes opposed to black, although this is how modern musicians are apt to regard it: except in the lowest octave, where it is ficta, B♭ is a recta note. Also, we shall see later (20) that because of its meaning in the Middle Ages an accidental does not necessarily result in a change in pitch. Only the raising or lowering of a note to create a pitch not in the recta gamut of Table I makes a ficta note.

9. *Semitones.* In the standard tuning of the Middle Ages, used by Ugolino, the tone was divided into unequal intervals, a larger and a smaller semitone: the latter occurs between mi and fa — between e & f, b♮ & c, between a & b♭; the larger semitone is represented in the normal gamut only between b♭ & b♮ and elsewhere always involves musica ficta notes, e.g., between f & f♯, e & e♭, etc. To put it concisely, at the top of an interval the sharp adds, the flat subtracts, a greater semitone: at the bottom of an interval the sharp subtracts, the flat adds, the greater semitone.

Perfection. An interval may be made perfect only by the addition of a greater semitone, thus the imperfect fifth is perfected by either a sharp on the top note or a flat on the lower. This alteration is the chief requirement and purpose of musica ficta: consonances must be made perfect, for philosophical as well as aural and aesthetic reasons.

Coloration. Philosophically, intervals immediately preceding perfect consonances ought to be as nearly perfect as possible. They ought therefore to be made as musically close to the perfect consonance as the vocabulary of the time allows, by expanding or contracting them chromatically as necessary. Such a procedure can hardly be called perfection, since only the consonances themselves can be completely perfect: Ugolino and others, however, often use the word *perficio* here, but surely in the true sense of making more complete, more nearly perfect. Sometimes instead of referring to the perfection of these intervals, the theorists say they are coloured, a word without the implications of the other term. The practice seems less obligatory than perfection itself.

The ambiguity in the meaning of the word *perficio* perhaps derives from a parallel confusion between the two interpretations of 'imperfect consonance'. On the one hand it may mean a diminished or augmented 'perfect' consonance such as an octave or fifth, which must be perfected; on the other, it can refer to those intervals which, in the fourteenth and fifteenth centuries, were neither fully consonant nor dissonant, that is, thirds and sixths, which ought to be brought closer to perfection. These, too, were 'imperfect consonances'. Which of the meanings is in question, and thus which meaning has to be given to *perficio*, is usually obvious from the context.

10. Ugolino refers only to harmonic aspects. He says nothing of correcting melodic tritones, nor of making returning-note figures semitones instead of tones, nor of augmented or diminished melodic intervals: in this he is in agreement with most major theorists, who deal with the topic principally from the vertical rather than the horizontal aspect. Implications, but not rules, about the melodic line may be drawn from the harmonic sequences, and also from the limitations inherent in the solmization system, which make awkward melodic intervals difficult to solmize, and also from Ugolino's hint that the horizontal lines of counterpoint follow the method (*ordinem*) of plainsong (sentences 1-5).

I first reproduce Albert Seay's edition of the original, retaining his sentence numbers[6]. The translation follows with the sentence numbers of the Latin placed at the beginning of paragraphs so that a parallel comparison may be made. In the translation, parentheses enclose the original Latin, where there might be some doubt as to the source of the English word. Brackets enclose editorial additions. Asterisks refer to the notes given after the text. Dots of omission appear only where the passage is absolutely repetitious and contains nothing new, or where the precise constitution of an interval in tones and semitones is set out in meticulous detail.

6. I should like to thank Professor Seay and Dr. Armen Carapetyan for their permission to reprint the chapter, published in *Declaratio Musicae Disciplinae*, ed. A. Seay, *Corpus Scriptorum de Musica* 7, 3 vols., Rome 1959-1962, II, pp.44-53. Seay's footnote variants are not included, being irrelevant here. The musical examples are reproduced only in the translation and the necessary reference is added to the Latin text. Obvious typographical errors are corrected.

CAPITULUM XXXIV

[1] *De ficta musica*

[2] Omnium vocum in suis consonantiis et dissonantiis demonstratione ostensa, quia contrapunctus cantus plani ordinem sequitur, et aliquando in sequendo et in notas recte et vere pronuntiando perfectae non possunt fieri consonantiae, sed imperfectae quae recto non conveniunt contrapuncto. [3] Idcirco ut quae sunt consonantiae imperfectae perficiantur, inventa est a philosophis musicis musica quaedam, quae ficta vocabulo nuncupatur. [4] Dicitur enim ficta, eo quod talis musica in eo loco ponitur ubi per se non est, sed fingitur in ipso esse, ut consonantiarum et dissonantiarum imperfectio compleatur, ut dictum est. [5] Imperfectiones autem consonantiarum quam plurimis reperiuntur in locis in quibus talis musicae fictio permaxime necessaria est, et est ibi talis fictio necessaria ubi alicuius consonantiae imperfectio reperiatur. [6] Reperitur enim primo diapente imperfectio a ♮ primo quadro ad F primum, est enim eorum quinta imperfecta, quae si debet ex contrapuncto perfici musica ficta mediante perficitur. [7] Ut verbi gratia, si tenor incipiens in primo A in re tonum intendat ad ♮ in mi, superior cum A et re in A secundo conveniat in la, quae eius re octava est, et cum mi conveniat in F primo, in fa quae eius mi quinta est, tunc inter mi et fa maxima ex quintae imperfectione oritur discordia, ex defectu enim semitonii maioris quod apotome nominatur. [8] Haec quinta redditur imperfecta, ob hanc enim considerationem et causam hac in parte musica ficta inventa est, cuius initium, id est, ut in D primo est locatum et fa in G primo positum. [9] Cuius mi in F, mi in ♮ inferiori in diapente perfecto dicitur respondere, ut patet inferius. [10] Merito igitur talis ficta musica est necessaria, quae potest tali descriptione declarari. [11] Musica ficta est alicuius vocis in loco ubi per se non est ad consonantiae perfectionem [*Seay*: perfectionum] necessaria positio.

[12] Ex hac enim descriptione primo intelligimus quod musica ficta ubi ponitur, ibi per se penitus non invenitur; secundo, quod musica ficta permittitur ut imperfectae consonantiae perficiantur; tertio, intelligimus quod musica ficta nisi necessitate cogente penitus non utamur.

[13] Secundo haec ficta necessaria ponitur a ♮ quadro secundo ad F secundum, ibi enim diapente imperfectio reperitur quod musicae fictae virtute perficitur, ut si tenor in prima A cum re tonum intendat ad ♮, re mi, superior in tertio A cum la diphtonum remittat ad F, la fa, tunc fa cum mi diapente sonat imperfectionem, et ideo fictae musicae necessaria est

positio, cuius fa in G secundo locatur, et ut eius initium in D secundo, ubi igitur erat per rectam musicam fa cum mi diapente sonans imperfectionem, est per fictam musicam mi cum mi ipsius diapente faciens perfectionem, ut hic utriusque perfectionis et imperfectionis exemplo patet demonstratio:

[14] Recta musica cum diapente imperfectione.
[15] Ficta musica cum diapente perfectione. Ex. 1, p. 30.
[16] Recta musica cum diapente imperfectione.
[17] Ficta musica diapente perfectione.

[18] Ex hac ficta musica superiori diapente imperfectio additur semitonium maius ex quo perfectum redditur diapente.

[19] Similiter ficta musica est adhibenda ubi superior per B molle cantaret et fa B mollis diapente inferius responderet; [20] tunc enim per rectam musicam mi inferius in E, fa superiori in B dicitur respondere, unde imperfectum sequitur diapente. [21] Necessario igitur pro habenda diapente perfectione ibi ficta musica ponitur, cuius fa in E ponitur et ut in ♮ primo locatur.

[22] Praeterea si superior cantus per B molle esset compositus, cuius fa nota inferior per diapason responderet, tunc per rectam musicam mi inferius fa superiori respondere contingeret, ex quo diapason imperfectio proveniret, et ideo ibi ficta musica est necessaria, cuius fictae musicae fa in ♮ primo ponitur et eius ut ante Γ fundatur, quorum exemple hic demonstrata patent:

[23] Recta musica cum diapente imperfectione.
[24] Ficta musica cum diapente perfectione. Ex. 2, p. 30.
[25] Recta musica cum diapason imperfectione.
[26] Ficta musica cum diapason perfectione.

[27] Similibus modis in manu musicali pro consonantiarum perfectione musicam fictam oportet accipere, ubi consonantiae altera pars alteri imperfecta respondet, sive sit diapente sive diapason, sive diapason diapente, sive bisdiapason in altera suarum partium in altero suorum extremorum imperfectum existens. [28] Ex musica igitur ficta imperfecta et inconsonans consonantia redditur; consonans et perfecta est ergo necessaria, ut dictum est, et ex hac ficta musica inferiori comprehendimus diapente et diapason, quae imperfecta ex se sunt, perfectionem accipere, quae in semitonii maioris additione consistit.

[29] Signa autem ut hic considerantur hanc fictam musicam demonstrativa sunt B molle sive rotundum, cui haec vox fa dicitur deservire, et ♮ quadrum sive durum, cui haec vox mi penitus famulatur, ubicumque igitur B molle reperimus, ibi immediatem notam fa proferimus, ubi vero ♮ quadrum sive durum, cui haec vox mi invenimus, ibi mi penitus annuntiamus. [30] Sunt ergo signa fictae musicae B et ♮, notae vero fa et mi, quae omnino, ut dictum est, pro consonantiarum terminis penitus repelluntur, ut in primo libro ubi de B molli et de ♮ quadro tractatur plenius dictum est. [31] Numquam igitur pro perfecta exprimenda consonantia quacumque mi

profertur contra fa, quia vel defectus in consonantia sequitur vel augmentum, ut dictum est, quorum utrumque quia consonantiae proportionem destruit, eius sonoritatis perfectionem impedit.

32 Ex superioribus fictae musicae demonstrationibus et exemplis in gravibus et acutis musicam fictam intelleximus habere locum. 33 Quae musica ficta ut praefertur fieri permittitur, ut si forte consonantiae inconsonae et imperfectae sint ad bonas et consonantes reducantur sonoritates, quia in contrapuncto consonantiae semper debent esse perfectae.

34 Sed talem musicam etiam in consonatiis imperfectis sive dissonantiis colorandis fingimus, causa vero fictionis huiusmodi duplex est, scilicet, causa harmoniae dulcioris habendae, et causa propinquioris perfectionis acquirendae; causa harmoniae dulcioris est quia nulli dubium est intelligenti et theorico quod ex fictione huiusmodi tum B mollis, tum ♮ quadri secundum subiectam cantus materiam facta dulcissima provenit auribus harmonia; causa vero propinquioris acquirendae perfectionis est quia cum omnis consonantia imperfecta sive dissonantia tamquam imperfectum quoddam suam appetat perfectionem et perfici, et tanto citius perficiatur quanto sit illi propinquior perfectioni. 35 Hinc est quod his dissonantiis huiusmodi signa ficta musicae praeponuntur, tum B molle, tum ♮ quadrum, ut harum praepositione dissonantiae ex minori distantia suam quam cupiunt acquirant perfectionem. 36 Sunt enim dissonantiae maiores et minores quarum tamen quae maior est pro perfectione habenda propinquius fit minor et quae minor maior. 37 Maioritas autem haec et minoritas atque differentia inter B atque ♮ sola maioris semitonii quantitate discernitur ut pluries dictum est, et his patet exemplis:

38 Primum exemplum demonstrationis. } Ex. 3a & b, pp. 31-32.
39 Secundum exemplum demonstrationis.

40 In his demonstratis exemplis causas fictionis musicae fictae comprehendimus, quas B et ♮ clare demonstrant; demonstrant enim B et ♮ perfectionem quam faciunt dissonantiis imperfectis et dulcem harmoniam eisdem quam tribuunt. 41 Nam ♮ quadrum in primo exemplo demonstrationis positum pro [*Seay*: per] quod eo in spatio dicitur mi notam, cui servit in eodem spatio positam sextam maiorem facit cum nota tenoris in A primo locata, quae absque ♮ quadri virtute minor sexta antea vocabatur tribus connexa tonis semitoniisque duobus; nunc autem ex quo eo in loco dicitur mi redditur, sexta suae immediatae consonantiae et perfectioni, scilicet, octavae conveniens, quae ex quatuor tonis unoque semitonio tantum connectitur eoque modo ♮ quadrum in exempli primi fine locatum penultimam dicitur perficere notam suae inferiori sextae correspondentem, ut intelligenti terminos metienti clarissime constat.

42 Primum vero B molle in exemplo primo locatum non dissonantiae perfectionem sed colorationem eius atque cum suae formae diminutione etiam eius immediatae perfectioni propinquiorem et immediatam adhae-

sionem ostendit, nam semoto B quadro [*Seay*: molli] dicimus re mi quae tonum efficiunt, cum B [*Seay*: molli *omitted*] autem dicimus mi fa quae semitonium faciunt. [43] Sed minor est distantia semitonii a sua praedicta consonantia et perfectione quam distantia toni et quanto minor est distantia tanto facilior est perfectio. [44] Igitur praedictum B non perfectionis causa ut perficiat, sed propinquioris adhaesionis ad suam perfectionem habendam, ut coloretur sexta ibi ponitur ratione.

[45] Similiter B rotundum secundum in primo exemplo ponitur nam eo nota E [*Seay*: B] serviens in linea cum sequenti semitonium constituunt, quae sine B [i.e., rotundum] tonum componunt, sed per semitonium minus distat dicta nota ab unisono immediate cum tenore sequente, et immediatius ei coniungitur quam per tonum, igitur, et cetera.

[46] B molle quod in superiori secundo exemplo in linea ponitur ad dissonantiae colorem atque eius propinquiorem adhaesionem ad suam immediate sequentem consonantiam, scilicet, unisonum, ponitur, quia ex ipsius B locatione sequitur a sua nota ad sequentem semitonii minoris positio in unisono suae tenoris notae respondens, sicut in primo exemplo de secundo B molli dictum est.

[47] Ex primo ♮ quadro in superiori secundo exemplo posito duo dicuntur necessario convenientia sequi; primum est distantia parva semitonii a nota praedente ipsum ♮ ad sequentem in diapente perfecto tenoris notae correspondentem. [48] Ex quo diapente nota ♮ praecedens videtur perfici. [49] Secundum est ex his dulcis proveniens harmonia, ut intelligenti patet.

[50] ♮ secundum quadrum in superiori secundo exemplo positum ea ibidem esse dicitur ratione qua ultimum ♮ quadrum in primo exemplo. [51] ♮ primum quadrum in secundo tenore positum est ut nota sibi serviens per minoris semitonii distantiam a sequente unisono perficiatur, sed B sequens molle notatur, ut eius nota cum sibi superius respondente perfectam valeant efficere sextam.

[52] Cognovimus ergo ex praemissis musicae fictae necessitatem consonantiarum perfectionem ac dissonantiarum colorationem, harmoniarum amoenitatem producentem, et quia haec musica ex eo dicitur ficta, quia ibi ponitur seu fingitur ubi per se non est, ideo duplicem manum invenimus, ubi omnes rectae musicae atque fictae voces ordinatae ponuntur, prima namque manus sub Γ immediate initium habet in F, cuius ordo vocum hic

est ordinate descriptus:

53 E														la
D													la	sol
C												la	sol	fa
B♭											la	sol	fa	mi
A										la	sol	fa	mi	re
G									la	sol	fa	mi	re	ut
F									sol	fa	mi	re	ut	
E								la	fa	mi	re	ut		
D							la	sol	mi	re	ut			
C						la	sol	fa	re	ut				
B♭					la	sol	fa	mi	ut					
A				la	sol	fa	mi	re						
G			la	sol	fa	mi	re	ut						
F			sol	fa	mi	re	ut							
E		la	fa	mi	re	ut								
D	la	sol	mi	re	ut									
C	sol	fa	re	ut										
♭	fa	♮-mi	ut			[*Seay*: fa ut ♮ mi]								
A	mi	re												
Γ	re	ut												
F	ut													

Cf. Table IIa, p. 34.

54 Haec namque manus his vocibus nuncupatur: [*slightly rearranged from Seay's diagram.*]

55 F	ut								
Γ	re		ut						
A	re		mi						
♭	fa		ut	♭	mi				
C	fa		ut		sol	re			
D	la		sol		re	mi	ut		
En	fa	E	la		mi	re	ut		
F	fa		ut		sol	mi	re		
G	sol		re		ut	la	mi	fa	
A	la		mi		re	sol	fa		
B	fa	♭	mi		ut	la	sol		
C	sol		fa		ut	re	la		
D	la		sol		re	mi	ut		
En	fa	E	la		mi	re	ut		
F	fa		ut		sol	mi	re		
G	sol		re		ut	la	mi	fa	
A	la		mi		re	sol	fa		
B	fa	♭	mi		la	sol			
C	sol		fa		la				[la, *omitted, completes the hexachord on E*]
D	la		sol						
E	la								

Cf. Table IIb, p. 35.

56 Aliam fictae musicae manum atque rectae invenimus a Γ inferius per diapente distantem, et in C incipientem a prima parum excepta gravitate distantem, quae tali est ordine in vocibus constituta:

57 E														la
D													la	sol
C													sol	fa
B♮												la	fa	mi
A											la	sol	mi	re
G										la	sol	fa	re	ut
F										sol	fa	mi	ut	
E									la	fa	mi	re		
D								la	sol	mi	re	ut		
C								sol	fa	re	ut			
B♮							la	fa	mi	ut				
A						la	sol	mi	re					
G					la	sol	fa	re	ut					
F					sol	fa	mi	ut						
E				la	fa	mi	re							
D			la	sol	mi	re	ut							
C			sol	fa	re	ut								
♮		la	fa	mi	ut									
A	la	sol	mi	re										
Γ	sol	fa	re	ut										
F	fa	mi	ut											
E	mi	re												
D	re	ut												
C	ut													

Cf. Table III, p. 36.

58 Et ex his multiplicatis vocibus atque fictis comprehendimus musicam fictam ubique posse constitui atque fingi praeterquam in E et A omnes enim aliae litterae his exceptis omnium sex vocum principium videntur habere, etiam comprehendimus quod sub Γ possunt multae voces imaginari et intelligi, scilicet, tertiae, quintae, sextae, octavae, decimae et duodecimae, et cetera, licet hic sint voces determinatae in C.

59 Antiqui autem huius fictae musicae veram cognitionem habentes quorum veritas modernis cantoribus penitus ignota manet in suae musicae veritate seu fictione, sive pro colorandis consonantiis sive pro eis ad maioritatem vel minoritatem reducendis duo signa, id est, duo b ♮, quorum alterum cum corpore rotundo primum, alterum cum corpore quadro secundum peni-

tus invenerunt, primum quidem signum, id est, b rotundum sive molle, sive in linea sive in spatio repertum erat, fa vocem significabat. [60]Secundum vero signum, id est, ♮ quadrum vel durum, ubi ponebatur mi vocem annuntiabat.

[61] Inventa sunt ergo praedicta signa primo pro consonantiis colorandis, ut ex ipsa consonantia colorata dulcior proveniat harmonia, quod fit quando maior consonantia ad minoritatem reducitur. [62] Secundo ipsa signa sunt inventa ut conso antiae imperfectae huiusmodi mediantibus signis ad earum perfectionem maioritatemque ducantur. [63] Ut autem ex huiusmodi ficta musica dulcior proveniat harmonia, sic potest exemplariter demonstrari, nam si gratia exempli fiat tenoris ascensus ab ut primi G ad re secundi A, ita quod ut re ascendendo tonum constituant, et fiat superioris descensus a mi ♮ secundi ad re secundi A quae mi et re etiam tonum faciant, tunc inter mi et ut diphtonus est, qui tertia maior est, quae, tertia non maior sed minor debet esse per regulam contrapuncti quae superius data est, quod si tertia per unisonum perficiatur quod illa tertia debet esse minor, et ut illa tertia sit minor oportet mutare diphtonum in semidiphtonum, quod fit si in spatio ubi est mi ponatur b rotundum quod significat fa, et tunc in spatio dicetur fa et in linea proxima descendenti, ubi est A secundum, dicetur mi, et sic de mi re, quea erant tonus, factae sunt fa mi, quae sunt semitonium minus; tonus autem excedit semitonium minus per semitonium maius, et sic illa tertia quae erat maior B molli mediante per subtractionem semitonii maioris facta est minor, quia diphtonus mutatus est in semidiphtonum qui semidiphtonus a diphtono per maius semitonium superatur, et ex hac maioris semitonii subtractione ac diphtoni in semidiphtonum mutatione dulcior consurgit harmonia, quam si talis semitonii subtractio et diphtoni mutatio non fieret.

[64] Pro consonantiis imperfectis sive dissonantiis perficiendis haec signa ut praefertur etiam sunt inventa, quoniam secundum regulam superius datam consonantiae et dissonantiae in contrapuncto debent esse perfectae et maiores et non minores et imperfectae, et ideo quando imperfectae reperiuntur aliquo praedictorum [*Seay*: praedictorem] signorum perficiuntur, ut verbi gratia tale ponatur exemplum in sexta minori sive imperfecta, descendat enim tenor faciens tonum ab E primo ad D primum mi re, superior autem ascendat a secundo C ad secundum D, faciens etiam tonum fa sol; a mi igitur primi E ad fa secundi C est sexta minor sive imperfecta composita ex tribus tonis et duobus minoribus semitoniis; est enim diapente cum semitonio quae sexta debet esse maior composita ex quatuor tonis et uno semitonio minore, quae vocatur diapente cum tono. [65] Cui sextae imperfectae si debeat perfici ei semitonii maioris debet fieri additio.

[66] Sed antiqui hanc sextam minorem et imperfectam ad sui maioritatem et perfectionem hoc modo videbantur reducere; nam in ipso C ubi est fa ponebant mi et sic ubi est recte fa ficte ponebant mi, et ante ipsum mi in ipsa linea ponebant ♮ quadrum quo ipsum mi habet significari, et in ipso

D ubi est verum sol ponebant fictum fa, ita quod in C et D ubi sunt verae fa sol quae tonum efficiunt ponebantur fictae mi fa quae semitonium faciunt, et sic dicebant isti quod per talem fictionem seu mutationem nominis et vocis reducitur talis sexta minor ad maioritatem et perfectionem, et quod reducatur talis sexta minor per tale signum, scilicet, ♮ quadrum, ad maioritatem sic quidam ostendunt, nam dicunt quod ascendendo a fa ad sol in cantu superiori ascendimus tonum, sed si loco de fa fingamus mi ut nobis ostenditur per signum antepositum tunc ordinate ascendendo loco de sol fingemus fa voce non mutate, et sic ascendemus semitonium minus cum a mi ad fa semper sit semitonium minus, quare elevabimus vocem supra verum fa per unum semitonium maius quod est a vero fa ad fictum mi, quoniam si a vero fa ad sol sit tonus et a ficto mi ad fictum fa sit semitonium minus necessario a vero fa ad fictum mi erit semitonium maius, et sic addetur illud semitonium maius ad illam sextam minorem quare per hanc additionem maior efficietur, ut esse debet cum maior minorem non excedat nisi per semitonium maius. [67] Haec illi.

[68] Sed pro dictorum confirmatione aliam forte clariorem reddimus rationem, et dicimus quod illud fictum ♮ quadrum significans mi positum in C facit illam sextam minorem esse maiorem, et quod faciat probatur sic. [69] Illa sexta dicitur esse maior, quae ex quatuor tonis et uno semitonio minore dicitur esse composita, sed illa sexta quae est minor, scilicet, a mi gravi ad fa acutum per appositionem fictae vocis mi est composita ex quatuor tonis et uno minore semitonio, igitur est maior. [70] Minor [*Seay*: Maior] est per se nota et maior [*Seay*: minor] probatur, nam mi quod ficte ponitur in C et fa quod ficte ponitur in D suum initium et fundamentum, scilicet, ut, habent in A secundo. [71] Unde per hanc fictam musicam in A dicimus ut, in B♮ re, in C mi, et cetera. [72] Igitur ab E primo ad C secundum per hanc fictam musicam est sexta maior et perfecta habens quatuor tonos et unum tantum semitonium minus, ut patet intelligenti, igitur, et cetera.

[73] Praeterea sexta maior excedit minorem per semitonium maius, sed haec sexta per hanc fictam musicam ab E ad C est maior, ut nunc probatum est, et ipsa sexta per veram musicam est minor, igitur ipsa sexta per fictam musicam excedit aliam per semitonium maius. [74] Quomodo autem excedat sic declaratur, nam si per veram musicam per ♮ quadrum acutum a ♮ ad C dicimus mi fa, quod est semitonium minus, et per hanc fictam musicam a ♮ ad C dicimus re mi, quod est tonus, cum tonus excedat semitonium minus per semitonium maius, sequitur quod in C inter fa et mi sit semitonium maius quo dicta sexta perficitur et additur ei ad eius perfectionem et per consequens ipsa sexta dicitur esse maior et perfecta, quod erat declarandum.

[75] Similes sextas, scilicet, maiorem et minorem, habemus a D primo ad B♮, nam si in B dicimus fa per B molle, tunc a D ad B habemus duo semitonia minora et tres tonos et per consequens sextam minorem. [76] Si

autem in ♮ dicimus mi per ♮ quadrum tunc unum tantum semitonium minus habemus et quatuor tonos et per consequens sextam maiorem. [77] Hanc autem differentiam ex fine ipsius sextae cognoscimus, nam finis sextae si fiat per B molle ab A ad B tunc erit minus semitonium mi fa. [78] Si autem fiat per ♮ quadrum tunc erit tonus re mi, cum autem tonus excedat semitonium minus per semitonium maius, sequitur quod inter hanc vocem mi ♮ quadri et hanc vocem fa B mollis, sit semitonium maius, quia si inter mi et fa est semitonium minus et inter re et mi est tonus, sequitur quod inter fa et mi in B♮ sit semitonium maius, quo sexta a D ad B♮ perficitur, et sic sexta minor erit per B molle, maior vero per ♮ quadrum.

[79] Similiter de hac musica in C, cuius initium est in A, possumus dicere quoniam si per veram musicam a ♮ ad C est semitonium minus mi fa, per hanc fictam musicam ab eodem ♮ ad C est tonus re mi qui minus semitonium excedit per maius, sequitur quod inter fa et mi in ipso C est semitonium maius quo dicta sexta ab E ad ipsum C maior efficitur et perfecta.

[80] His itaque sic declaratis, dicimus quod ficta musica ad cantus necessitatem eiusque ornatum atque decorem inventa est, et quia haec musica ficta de qua agitur cuius signum ponitur in C secundo cum mi suum principium, id est, suum ut, habet in A secundo, ideo dictum principium, id est, ipsum ut, in suprascriptis contrapuncti manibus ubi non est debet collocari ut in ipso C valet sexta maior reperiri.

12 *Ugolino of Orvieto: Declaratio Music Discipline About Musica Ficta*

1-5 All the notes and the consonances and dissonances produced by them have been demonstrated. And because counterpoint follows the [solmizing?] method (*ordinem*) of plainsong, sometimes perfect consonances cannot be produced by true and normal (*recta*) pronunciation [of the solmization syllables], causing imperfect consonances which are not suitable to proper counterpoint. To perfect such imperfect consonances theoreticians (*philosophis musicis*) evolved a certain music called musica ficta, so called because it is placed in a position where it does not exist in its own right (*per se*, i.e., in recta music) but is imagined. It is used to fill out imperfect consonances and dissonances. Wherever the former occur musica ficta is quite obligatory (*permaxime necessaria*), and where it is obligatory the imperfection of some consonance is found.

6-9 & 13-18* The [vertical] fifth B-F, solmized by musica recta, is imperfect because the interval between mi and fa lacks the greater semitone and an extreme discord arises (Ex. 1a). This must be perfected by adding the greater semitone to the upper note (*superiori*) of the fifth, which is brought about through musica ficta by means of the hexachord (*in parte*, sentence 8; *positio*, sentence 13) whose beginning, ut, is placed on D: its fa is on G and its mi on F[♯] and the latter forms a perfect fifth with the mi below (Ex. 1b):

Ex. 1a 1b

10-12 Such an example demonstrates the necessity of musica ficta, the obligatory placing of a certain syllable (*vocis*) where it does not exist in musica recta, in order to perfect a consonance, and from the example we know... that we may use it only where absolutely necessary (*necessitate cogente penitus*).

13-18: see 6-9.

19-26 Similarly musica ficta has to be used when the upper part sings B♭ in the soft hexachord (*per B molle*) and the other voice sings the musica recta mi a fifth or an octave lower, producing either an imperfect fifth or octave. In both cases a musica ficta fa is placed instead of the recta mi: in the former case this is done through the hexachord whose ut is on B♭, in the latter through the one whose ut is on the F below gamma:

Ex. 2

27-28 Where one part of the consonance harmonises imperfectly with the other — at the 5th, 8ve, 12th or 15th, etc. — it is proper to use musica ficta, and from the previous examples we can see that the greater semitone may [also] be added to the lower note (*inferiori*) of the interval in order to restore the necessary perfection.

29-33 The signs designed to display musica ficta are ♭, to which we immediately utter the subservient syllable fa, and ♮, to which we pronounce mi, and these signs of fa and mi are wholly and utterly rejected as simultaneous extremes for the same consonance: thus mi is never solmized against fa on a perfect consonance, because thereby the interval is either too small or too large, both of which defects destroy the proportion and hinder the perfection of its sound*. We now see where musica ficta is placed, in both high and low registers, and that it is permitted in order to correct imperfect and unconsonant consonances, since these ought always to be perfect in counterpoint.

34-39 But the reason for ficta is twofold: in order to have sweeter harmony on imperfect consonances [i.e., to perfect them completely] and also in order to colour a dissonant interval to bring it closer to perfection. The former cannot be doubted by any intelligent and knowledgeable man because, by adding either the ♭ or ♮ — according to the accompanying melodic line of the music (*subiectam cantus materiam*) — a most sweetly made harmony arises for the ears. The second reason is that, just as every imperfect thing tries to reach perfection, so every imperfect consonance or dissonance should approach perfection as closely as possible, and by as much as they are altered (*perficiatur*) by so much will they be closer to perfection. Therefore either ♭ or ♮ is placed in front of dissonances of this kind so that those which desire it may acquire perfection to the extent by which they differ from the uninflected pitch (*ex minori distantia.*) For there are both major and minor intervals which are dissonant and in order to take on perfection the major is made minor and vice versa. And the difference between a major and minor interval, as well as the only difference between b♭ and b♮, lies in the greater semitone, as stated several times, and as shown by these examples:

Ex. 3a

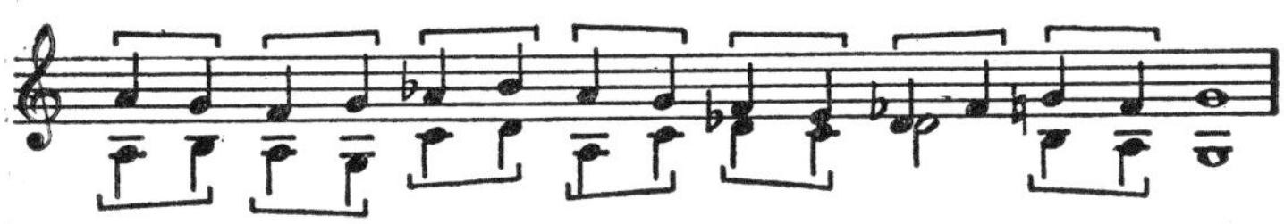

40-46 Here we see the reasons for musica ficta shown by ♭ and ♮, which illustrate the perfection they make out of imperfect dissonances and the sweet harmony they bestow upon them. In Ex. 3a the ♮ [i.e., ♯] is placed so that mi is said on the f, making a major sixth with the note a in the tenor where there was previously a minor sixth. The sixth is made major to render it suitably close to the nearest (*immediatae*) consonance and perfection, the following octave: the ♮ is said to perfect [i.e., to bring the interval closer to perfection] the interval of a sixth (*notam suae inferiori sextae correspondentem*). This appears most clearly to the intelligent man who considers the extremities [of the interval]. In the same example the first ♭ is placed not to perfect a dissonance but to colour it, and by replacing the tone, re-mi, with a semitone, mi-fa, from the $^{a}_{a}$ to the $^{b}_{b}$, the sixth is made minor and reveals that it is as close as possible in size and position (*propinquiorem et immediatam adhaesionem*) to the nearest (*immediatae*) perfection [i.e., the octave As]. In so far as the semitone is closer than the tone to perfection, by so much is the perfecting [of the sixth] easier. The ♭ is therefore placed to colour the sixth, not to perfect it but to bring it closer to the following perfection. The second ♭ in Ex. 3a is placed for a similar reason, so that the third, c-e, is a semitone closer to the immediately following unison with the tenor, etc.* The same is true of the first ♭ [in the upper voice] of Ex. 3b.

* This note should be B

47-51 The first ♮ in the upper voice of Ex. 3b is necessary for two reasons: the first is to make the step f-e [previously made e♭] a semitone so that the note preceded by the ♮ makes a perfect fifth with the note of the tenor, the second reason is the sweeter harmony which results. The other ♮ in the upper voice occurs for the same reason as the last ♮ of Ex. 3a. The ♮ in the tenor of Ex. 3b is placed so that the third, b-d, is a semitone closer to the perfection of the following unison, and the following b is preceded by a ♭ so that it may make a major sixth with the note above*.

52-58. We know from what has been said that the perfecting of consonances, the colouring of dissonances and the production of sweeter harmony makes musica ficta necessary and that it is so called because it is placed or imagined where it does not exist in musica recta (*per se*). Because of this we devise a double [Guidonian] hand, on which all the syllables of recta and ficta are placed in well-ordered fashion. The first hand begins on the F immediately below gamma, and the order of syllables is shown in Table IIa*. We would solmize the notes as shown in Table IIb*. Another hand of recta and ficta music, beginning on the C a fifth lower than gamma, differs from the first by little except its low pitch. Its order of notes is shown in Table III*. We see that below gamma many notes (*voces*) may be imagined and understood, 3rds, 5ths, 8ves, 10ths, 12ths, etc.: therefore it is permitted that the syllables (*voces*) be determined from C. And from this multitude of ficta syllables we understand that musica ficta [hexachords] may be established and imagined anywhere except on E and A, for all pitches other than these evidently may serve for the beginning, [ut], of a hexachord†.

59-65 However, in the recta or ficta of their music, whether for perfection or colouring, modern singers are ignorant of the truth of the ancients, who, having a sure knowledge of this musica ficta, devised the ♭ and ♮ to signify the syllables fa and mi. These signs were invented so that the colouring of intervals (*consonantiis*) produces a sweeter harmony, which occurs when a major interval is reduced to a minor one [and vice versa], and so that imperfect consonances are made larger (*ad... maioritatem*) and perfect. The sweeter harmony which arises is shown in this example [abstracted from the verbal text]:

not B-mi A-re / G-ut A-re but B♭-fa A-mi / G-ut A-re. Because of the rule of counterpoint given above, the third ought to be minor when it is completed (*perficiatur* — i.e., perfected) by a following unison. It is made minor by placing the ♭ to give fa-mi, the lesser semitone, instead of mi-re, a tone. The tone is a greater semitone larger than the lesser semitone, and thus the major third is made minor by the subtraction of the greater semitone: in other words, the ditonus is changed into a semiditonus, making a sweeter harmony. Since, according to the rule given above, consonances and dissonances in counterpoint ought to be perfect and major, not imperfect or minor*, when imperfect ones occur they have to be altered by one of the signs already mentioned. For example, this next sixth ought to be not c-fa d-sol / E-mi D-re but c♯-mi d-fa: / E-mi D-re to bring it closer to the perfection [of the following octave] the greater semitone ought to be added.

TABLE IIa

	Hexachords on G, C & F, producing the normal, recta gamut.		Hexachords on F, B♭ & E♭, producing the same gamut transposed down a tone, as under a signature of B♭ & E♭.	Hexachords on D.		Hexachord on low F, and on B♮ & E♮, producing ficta pitches.	Hexachords on D.
ee	l						
dd	l-s						
					cc♯	l	
cc	s-f		l				
♮♮	m			l		s	l
♭♭	f		s				
aa	l-m-r			s		f	s
		aa♭	f		g♯	l-m	
g	s-r-u		l-m	f			f
		f♯		m	f♯	s-r	m
f	f-u		s-r				
e	l-m			r		f-u	r
		e♭	f-u		d♯	m	
d	l-s-r		m	u			u
					c♯	l-r	
c	s-f-u		l-r				
♮	m			l		s-u	l
♭	f		s-u				
a	l-m-r			s		f	s
		a♭	f		G♯	l-m	
G	s-r-u		l-m	f			f
		F♯		m	F♯	s-r	m
F	f-u		s-r				
E	l-m			r		f-u	r
		E♭	f-u		D♯	m	
D	s-r		l-m	u		l	u
					C♯	r	
C	f-u		s-r			s	
♮	m					u	
		♭	f-u		♭	f	
A	r		m			m	
Γ	u		r			r	
		F	u		F	u	

TABLE IIb

ee	la
dd	la-sol
cc	sol-fa[-la]
bb	fa/ ♮♮ mi-la-sol
aa	la-mi-re-sol-fa
g	sol-re-ut-la-mi-fa
f	fa-ut-sol-mi-re
en	fa/ e la-mi-re-ut
d	la-sol-re-mi-ut
c	sol-fa-ut-re-la
b	fa/ ♮ mi-ut-la-sol
a	la-mi-re-sol-fa
G	sol-re-ut-la-mi-fa
F	fa-ut-sol-mi-re
En	fa/ E la-mi-re-ut
D	la-sol-re-mi-ut
C	fa-ut-sol-re
B	fa-ut/ ♮ mi
A	re-mi
Γ	re-ut
F	ut

TABLE III

	Hexachords on C, G & F, producing the normal, recta gamut.		Hexachords on low F & C, and on B♭, producing the same gamut transposed down a fifth, as under a signature of B♭.	Hexachords on D.		Hexachords on low F & C, and on B♮, producing ficta pitches.	Hexachords on D.
ee	l						
dd	l-s						
cc	s-f						
♮♮	m			l			l
♭♭	f						
aa	l-m-r			s			s
					g♯	l	
g	s-r-u		l	f			f
		f♯		m	f♯	s	m
f	f-u		s				
e	l-m			r		f	r
		e♭	f		d♯	m	
d	l-s-r		m	u			u
					c♯	r	
c	s-f-u		r				
♮	m			l		u	l
♭	f		u				
a	l-m-r			s			s
					G♯	l	
G	s-r-u		l	f			f
		F♯		m	F♯	s	m
F	f-u		s				
E	l-m			r		f	r
		E♭	f		D♯	m	
D	s-r		l-m	u		l	u
					C♯	r	
C	f-u		s-r			s	
♮	m			l		u	l
		♭	f-u		♭	f	
A	r		l-m	s		l-m	s
Γ	u		s-r	f		s-r	f
		F♯		m	F♯		m
		F	f-u		F	f-u	
		E	m	r	E	m	r
		D	r	u	D	r	u
		C	u		C	u	

66-67 The ancients thus corrected this sixth by replacing the recta fa on c with the ficta mi signified by ♮, causing fa to fall on d which was previously sol, and making a semitone instead of a tone: through such fiction and changing of the name and pitch the minor sixth is corrected. Ascending from c-fa to d-sol in the upper voice, we move up a tone, but if we put mi in the place of fa, as shown by the ♮, then we may imagine d-fa in the place of d-sol — in which case the pitch (*voce*) is unchanged. Thus we move up a lesser semitone, since from mi to fa is always a lesser semitone, and we raise the pitch (*vocem*) of the c above the true fa by one greater semitone, from the true fa to the ficta mi. For if true fa to sol is a tone, and ficta mi to fa is a lesser semitone, then true fa to ficta mi will necessarily be a greater semitone, whereby the minor sixth is made major.

68-74 To confirm these things, we present a clearer reason for saying that the ficta ♮-mi placed on the c makes the minor sixth major... The sixth in itself is minor, but is proved major when the ficta mi and fa placed on c and d have their foundation and beginning, ut, on the note a. In this hexachord we say ut on a, re on b♮, mi on c[♯], etc. So from E to c by this ficta hexachord is major and [more nearly] perfect. Through the semitone placed by musica ficta the major exceeds the minor sixth by the greater semitone, which is added [to intervals] for their perfection.

75-79 Similar sixths occur between D and b: if we say fa by B♭ the sixth is minor, if we say mi through the ♮ it is major, the former syllable standing a lesser semitone and the latter a tone from the note a-mi. And since the tone is a greater semitone larger than the lesser semitone, then between ♮-mi and ♭-fa is a greater semitone, etc. Similarly with the ficta on c whose hexachord begins on the note a, by which the sixth from E to c is made major.

80 Having stated these things, we say that musica ficta was contrived for the necessity of song (*cantus*) and for its ornamenting and beauty (*ornatum atque decorem*). And because the ficta in question, whose ♮-mi is placed on c, has its ut on a, then that ut, where it does not exist in the hands written above, ought to be arranged so that on the c in question the pitch is enough to make the sixth major*.

13 *Commentary*

* 6-9 & 13-18 These two sections discuss the same musical sequence, the latter transposing it an octave higher. There is a reason. In the lower octave the B♭ is not available by musica recta (see gamut on p. 18) and Ugolino, as usual choosing the upper rather than the lower part to alter, corrects the interval with F♯. In the higher octave a recta B♭ is available and would normally be the method of perfecting the fifth: in this case, however, a manuscript accidental ♮, still a recta note, is placed specifically

to exclude correction by recta ♭, making the f♯ obligatory. In both cases the F♯-mi is specified by indicating ♭-fa on the G.

* 29-33 Note the prohibition of *mi contra fa*, a combination which is forbidden only on consonances, not in general. This standard limitation of the rule, noted by Margaret Bent[7], has not been sufficiently emphasised. It cannot mean, as has been stated in print, a prohibition of dissonance in general. (See section 73).

* 40-46 Ugolino fails even to mention the third ♭ of Ex. 3a, the f♭ which is, in our present-day system, meaningless and unnecessary. In the medieval system it would return the fa from the e to the f pitch.

* 47-51 Ugolino does not state the reason why this sixth, which does not immediately precede a consonance, has to be major. He also fails to mention another accidental, the first ♭ in the tenor of Ex. 3b: this is doubly unfortunate since, in contrast to the one discussed under 40-46, no certain reason for its presence can be suggested even within the medieval system. There is no necessity to change hexachords since the notes up to the b♮ can be solmized sol-fa-sol-re-fa-mi in the hard hexachord alone. But in that case the b would be automatically ♮; Ugolino may have introduced the flat simply for this reason. Alternatively, it could be placed to give mi against mi rather than mi against re on the perfect fifth.

* 52-58 It is possible to interpret these Tables in two totally different ways, according to whether the ut of some of the ficta hexachords is placed on the fa or the mi of the ambiguous B of the recta system, i.e., on B♭ or B♮. Only the hexachord beginning on D, common to both Tables, is not affected by this ambiguity. Each Table shows both alternatives (rendering the D hexachord in each of the choices), separating the ficta from the recta syllables and choosing the fa of the recta system for the ut in the middle column, and the mi (recta) for ut in the last column. That both interpretations should exist is perhaps intentional. If the purpose is to show the ficta notes available, i.e., largely sharps, then the last column fulfils that function. But then the resulting pitches in Tables II & III are identical and there is no reason for having both diagrams. More likely is that the tables are not to show the ficta notes but the ficta hexachords and where they may begin in order to produce the ficta notes: of the two tables, each duplicates in the lower octave the recta hexachords on F & C, each has the hexachord on D, but the first has others on B and A, the second only on B. Their purpose in exposing hexachords rather than pitches is perhaps confirmed by sentence 58, marking the absence of hexachords built on E and A in Table III. These arguments favour the interpretation producing the last column. On the other hand, if the purpose is to show how complete ficta systems can be constructed, duplicating the recta gamut at the fifth and tone below

7. Bent, diss., 418-419. Cf. Jacobs, "Spanish Renaissance Discussion...", fn. 29.

— i.e., what would be produced by key-signatures of B♭ alone and of B♭ & E♭ — then the columns in the middle, which are more regular, conventional, and symmetrical, would serve. The latter interpretation is somewhat weakened by the unmistakable presence of the hexachord on D, which upsets the symmetry because it could not be produced by the suggested transpositions of the gamut. The clear separation, in Table IIb, of En-fa and E-la-mi-re-ut surely mirrors the B-fa/B-mi ambiguity of the untransposed gamut and the same distinction of pitch must be present. The other clear separation, in the same table, between B-fa-ut and B-mi implies ut on B♭, giving E♭-fa to confirm that En-♭-fa and E-♮-la-mi-re-ut are different pitches: the letter n probably indicates the natural hexachord into which E♭ falls in the transposition producing the middle column. E-♭-fa therefore confirms that column rather than the last. But if En-fa produces E-♭-fa, then E-la-mi-re-ut produces E-♮-ut, a note which occurs only in the last column and not in the middle one.

The attempt to mingle the two columns and to relate those of Table IIa to the syllables of Table IIb soon fails to work satisfactorily: for example, above C-ut the G must be sol and ♮, but above E-♮-ut the G must be mi and ♯ and to be consistent with the B-fa-ut/B-mi and E-fa/E-la-mi-re-ut distinction Table IIb should show G-sol-re-ut-la-fa/G-mi. The evidence is thus conflicting and does not render a firm decision possible. A commitment to one or the other version is probably unwise, in case the ambiguity is intentional. At the very least, it is evident that Ugolino is moving a stage beyond the mere production of ficta notes on the monochord and is attempting to organize them rationally in systems paralleling the normal one[8].

† 52-58 See note to 80.

* 59-65 Ugolino here simply forgets that thirds and sixths have to be made minor before unisons or fifths.

* 80 The stressing of the hexachord built on the note a is perhaps because this particular position is markedly omitted from both of the Tables given earlier. Although Ugolino also verbally notes the omission of the hexachord on E (sentence 58), Table I confirms its availability, on either E♮ or E♭.

8. In their attempts to organize musica ficta in the fifteenth century, theorists began to refer to the new hexachords as *coniunctae*, discussed by Albert Seay, "The 15th-Century *Coniuncta*...", and briefly in Bent, diss., 426-427. In his references to Ugolino in the former discussion, Seay makes no attempt to solve or even to refer to the problems of these Tables, but accepts without question the interpretation rendered in my middle column, with hexachords on B♭, D, and E♭.

14. Accidentals written into manuscripts of early music are not necessarily those of the composer. Indeed, often the majority were not his. Of the different stages involved in the production of a particular manuscript, only one, the composer's autograph, will contain his accidentals, whereas each successive copying or use of a source may well increase or diminish the amount of chromaticism written in, or may change it in some way, either by error or by intention. It is quite clear that scribes could have considerable say in the actual details of notation[9] and that performers may have made changes for reasons apparent only in rehearsal. Thus, which of the accidentals required in performance happen to have found their way into a particular source depends on a number of factors, including a) a scribe's willingness or reluctance to copy accidentals faithfully from his exemplar, b) his tendency to add accidentals on his own initiative, c) addition of accidentals by later users of the copy. Subsequent additions may not be compatible with the chromaticism that is already written in (58). Any permutation of these and other factors in any degree may arise during the transmission of a single piece and it is rarely possible to distinguish which factors are in operation.

A study of accidentals in detail is therefore complicated by the presence of different layers. It often seems, for example, that some accidentals are later additions, although it is rarely possible to state definitely how much later they may be. Only a thorough paleographical investigation of an original source can give reliable information; photographic reproductions can never show clearly the niceties of erasures, hair-lines, different colours of ink, and so on, upon which an intelligent assessment must be based. Indeed, sometimes symbols in the original do not appear at all in photographic copies, being lightly drawn, or small in size.

15. In most cases, then, we must work with a set of symbols whose precise relationship to each other and to the original music is not clear, and we should realise that some of our basic premises may be weak. There are some mitigating factors. For instance, medieval music sometimes became old-fashioned rather quickly and was discarded, at least in areas where composition flourished; we may assume from this that accidentals which appear to be of later

9. Bent, diss., *passim*.

date are probably no more than a decade or two distant. A period of time such as this may, it is true, be of immense importance, but the state of our knowledge of musica ficta principles is still so little refined that, even if we could distinguish layers of accidentals year from year, we should hardly be able to use that knowledge to alter our method of adding further accidentals. In any case, where musical styles were kept up to date and where older manuscripts were discarded, styles of ficta also must have changed, and perhaps each repertory of pieces has some integrity of composition and ficta style, regardless of internal layers of additions.

We may expect to find more consistency from the work of a single scribe concerned with one repertory, especially if that scribe shows the tendency to change on his own initiative. In addition, we may find some consistency within the work of a single composer. The present study is based on a source ideal for the purpose. The Old Hall MS has been the subject of detailed research in many areas, and for the new edition prepared by the author and Margaret Bent[10] the original book itself was examined minutely from all possible aspects. The results of this study, which was carried out by Mrs Bent, are admirably presented in her dissertation, "The Old Hall Manuscript, a Paleographical Study" (Cambridge, diss., 1968), in what must be one of the most comprehensive paleographical investigations of any early musical manuscript. I have examined the original only briefly, concerning myself almost exclusively with the accidentals. At the end of this study a complete list of all the manuscript accidentals, prepared by Margaret Bent, is given: it may be used to demonstrate the unreliability of microfilm or other reproductions.

16. There may be doubts about the relevance of Italian theory on ficta, such as that presented earlier, to an English practical source, especially since there is a noticeable absence of contemporary English references to the topic. But the theory producing recta and ficta notes and explaining accidentals was universal in the fourteenth and early fifteenth centuries, even though the desire to write about such matters may not have been common to all countries. In references to the specific application of musica ficta principles during the same period, there are no severe contradictions between theorists of different nationalities even though they may treat of the subject from opposing view-points such as those discussed (7). The isolated allusions to ficta by English theorists, Odington and the author

10. Published in 1970 by the American Institute of Musicology in Rome, *Corpus Mensurabilis Musicae* 46.

of *Quatuor Principalia* in particular[11], make good sense in conjunction with the more detailed accounts of Ugolino and Prosdocimus[12], and the treatises of some writers, such as Jean de Muris, were recopied and used in various countries many decades after their first composition. Thus, in this area, it is justified to regard most theorists of fourteenth and early fifteenth centuries as complementary rather than contradictory. But the style of practical music naturally changed and it would be unwise to treat all pieces of the period as equally susceptible to ficta. If a distinction is drawn it should be primarily between methods of composition rather than between pieces of different national origin. The chanson-style piece composed in England before 1420 or 1430 will be chromatically much the same as a contemporary French chanson and will be just as amenable to the same kind of alteration by additional accidentals: a descant composition is likely to require different treatment. Other variations may accrue from local or *ad hoc* preference, skill and conservatism, about which we have little knowledge. With respect to Old Hall specifically, there are strong signs of continental influence from both France and Italy, and its concordances were widely distributed in European countries. That performers of different nationalities did not find it difficult to apply their own kind of ficta suggests that there were common principles with sufficient flexibility to accommodate national peculiarities of style.

17. Old Hall is a carefully written source, containing a large repertory much of which was written down by a single scribe whose musical ability is attested by the changes and corrections he makes. For example, he erases and repositions some accidentals[13]; in the case of purely mechanical copying this should be necessary only in the case of a few definite errors. But apparently the specific position of an accidental often, if not always, had a purpose, and when the meaning or position was not clear to the scribe from his exemplar he himself changed the location. Probably some accidentals are scribally added, some are accurately copied from the exemplar, some are scribally changed. Once again, we can rarely be sure which is the case, and are presented with yet a further series of permutations. However, apparently unnecessary repositioning of an accidental indicates that the precise position of such symbols had some meaning known to the scribe. The few later additions in Old Hall which concern accidentals can be attributed to the other scribes of the book,

11. Odington: Coussemaker I, 182. "Quatuor Principalia": ibid. IV, 200.
12. Ugolino: ed. A. Seay. Prosdocimus: Coussemaker III, 193.
13. Bent, diss., 107. See section 42 of the present work.

working only a few years later, although at a time when styles had changed somewhat[14]. Within the work of the main scribe, scribe A, there occur groups of pieces by a single composer: Leonel Power's compositions form the largest body of such pieces and it is interesting to note that their chromaticism is frequently unusual. The character of the Old Hall manuscript therefore minimises the difficulties resulting from differences between composers' styles, from different scribal layers, from later additions by scribes or performers whose abilities and relevance are difficult to assess.

18. In the following pages I have restricted my examination of manuscript accidentals, mainly for practical reasons, to those in scribe A's pieces, omitting those which are incomplete (that is, lacking one or more parts throughout) and those which have major concordances. Much of the evidence for variable extempore additions relies on the differences between concordances, and the field is absorbing and enlightening. Examination of manuscript variants in this respect was largely irrelevant since the purpose was to establish the practice of a single source, Old Hall itself. Although one should heed Lowinsky's sensible warning not to draw general conclusions from the idiosyncracies of a single source, the principles evolved or suggested here could, I am sure, be applied, with the proper caution, to any source of the later fourteenth or early fifteenth century. Outside these few decades the methods of composition will be different enough for other criteria to apply: attempts to interpret or to add accidentals by the standards of one period to the music of another must surely be avoided as unwise and unlikely to succeed.

Within these limits is a body of some 700 to 800 Old Hall accidentals, sufficient to provide hints rather than proofs, especially as the exceptional piece, of which there are several, may produce misleading results in certain areas. For that reason few percentages have been quoted, and only really significant statistical differences have been used. Illustration by example also has its perils since the interesting passage shown may be the exception or the isolated error. As far as possible several occurences of the same feature have been found where a single instance is shown. References are to the piece number (of the modern Inventory, *Musica Disciplina* XXI, 1967, pp. 130-147) and to the folios in the manuscript: when a reference to a particular accidental and its position is given, this follows the method used in Appendix III, the List of Accidentals. In the examples I have observed as strictly as possible the exact

14. Bent, diss., *passim*.

placing of accidentals, which in some cases is of crucial importance. However, the reader should always consult the original since the chasm between it and modern transcription must frequently mislead (90). There are no editorial accidentals in the examples, but occasionally line changes in the original or other relevant features have been noted.

Symbols and their meaning

19. The actual symbols used in this period are as follows: a) the ♭, occasionally written with a double bow when referring to the octave signified by double letters (see p. 18). This sign occurs on B & E and rarely or with special meaning on A, D, G: b) the ♯ or ♮, sometimes elaborated with dots as in the Bologna Q 15 and Padua 1225 MSS (see Plate I), and occasionally in the shape of an h as in the Warsaw MS. The ♯ and ♮ versions are usually graphically indistinguishable. Although some theorists recognise a difference between them, for practical purposes there is no significance to be placed on the choice of one shape for the sign rather than another[15]. The use of ♮ as a universal cancelling sign is of modern origin, and in the Middle Ages this function was denoted by the ♭, to change a mi back to fa, or by ♮ or ♯ (mi) to cancel a ♭-fa. Alternatively some scribes use: c) the symbols f c g to cancel previous sharpening of those pitches. These are discussed under Cancellation (58).

20. Accidentals in the Middle Ages do not have the single, consistent effect we attribute to them nowadays, but rather have a single, consistent function which covers several different effects including our present one. By specifying the solmization syllable they indicate where semitones lie. These intervals always lie between mi and fa regardless of which hexachord is in use: thus the accidental is related to either mi or fa, the former below, the latter above the semitone. Following from this is the universal rule for interpreting accidentals according to medieval theory, a rule without variation up to the fifteenth century and later[16]. The version given is that of Prosdocimus, but compare Ugolino's sentences 29-33, 59-65: *wherever ♭ is placed we ought to call that sound fa, and wherever ♮ is placed we ought to call that sound mi, regardless of whether the note would or would*

15. Coussemaker III, 258. Bent, diss., 406-7. J. Wolf, "Geschichte der Mensural-Notation von 1250-1460", Leipzig 1904; photographic reprint published Hildesheim 1965, pp. 109-119. M. Gerbert, "Scriptores Ecclesiastici de Musica...", St. Blasien 1784; reprint Hildesheim 1962, p.89.
16. Bent, diss., 407-409.

not normally have those syllables (Coussemaker III, 198). I do not know of any theorist before the fifteenth century who refers to the lowering or raising of the pitch by the application of an accidental, although this effect — our modern one — is invariably one of those available in the medieval system. Prosdocimus elsewhere says *in a rising interval ♭ [on the upper note] diminishes the ascent and ♯ augments it* (Coussemaker III, 198), which is perhaps deliberately ambiguous, since when an ascending interval is diminished by a ♭ the effect may be achieved by either lowering the upper note or raising, i.e., sharpening, the lower note. Ugolino specifically indicates F♯ by placing a ♭ in the space above, on G (sentences 13-18, Ex. 1). Prosdocimus further says *these signs add or subtract no other interval than the greater semitone* (Coussemaker III, 198) without saying that the greater semitone *must* be added or subtracted: F♭ means F-fa without altering the pitch — it can never mean, as it would for us, the pitch E, which is only a lesser semitone from F. Ugolino, in sentence 66 incidentally implies the alteration of pitch without emphasising it: *we may imagine D-fa in place of D-sol — in which case the pitch is unchanged* indicates that the C-mi a semitone below D-fa must be raised in pitch to make C♯. Margaret Bent has found an explicit reference to alteration of pitch in another fifteenth century treatise (Bent, diss., 408). As the fifteenth century progresses, the emphasis on the modern, narrower meaning of accidentals must increase, as the medieval system and ideals become replaced by Renaissance principles. But for medieval manuscripts, the wider function for accidentals must be expressed by the medieval definition: a ♭ means fa, on a pitch standing a semitone above mi, an interval which can be achieved in three ways — a) by lowering the pitch so marked, b) by leaving the pitch unchanged, as on the note F, already a semitone above E, c) by raising the lower pitch. With the necessary modifications, the ♯ or ♮ has a similar set of interpretations, deriving from its meaning as mi, a semitone below fa. While it is impossible to tell what importance practising musicians of the time placed on each of these meanings, it is clear that for us to solve musica ficta problems satisfactorily we need normally consider only meaning a), which becomes the sole survivor. Accidentals resulting in b) occur normally on certain pitches, but since they do not call for the alteration of any note, we can ignore their immediate effect, although not the reason for their presence. Alternative c) we need consider only as a last resort, when no other interpretation or solution can reasonably be found. The wider meaning allowed to accidentals, and the placing of them in positions unnecessary or unusual in our system, where they have no apparent or immediate effect, must be taken into account and forms the basis for this study.

21. The syllables mi and fa represented by the accidentals occur on the following pitches in the standard gamut: B♮-mi, E-mi, A-mi and F-fa, B♭-fa, C-fa. These are all recta notes. Thus, where C♭, F♭, B♭, E♮-♯, A♮-♯, B♮-♯ are so marked they are part of the recta gamut and do not belong to the musica ficta series, even though they call for the use of an accidental. It is therefore not correct to equate accidentals and musica ficta.

22. Medieval practice, as well as theory, used the recta gamut with its hexachords and syllables as the basis for learning and teaching music: the pronunciation of the syllables was a means, perhaps the only one, of insuring that the correct notes were sung. If the accidental serves to indicate where mi and fa lie, then in a broader sense it serves to show which of the hexachords is in use, since knowing the position of the semitone makes sense only in the wider melodic context of the whole hexachord.

23. One of the points not explicit about the meaning of accidentals is whether the B♭-fa always refers to the soft hexachord, and B♮-mi always to the hard. One theorist relates the ♯ to the hard and ♮ to the natural hexachord (see Bent, diss., 407), but this further distinction seems purely academic. Most writers call ♭ and ♮ ♭-*rotundum sive molle* and ♮-*quadratum sive durum*, suggesting that the soft and hard hexachords are always implied. But these are just traditional names reflecting the fact that the symbols ♭ and ♮ originally occurred only on the note B of soft and hard hexachords respectively. Ugolino, for example, uses the words *B rotundum* for E♭ and the *B quadratum* sign ♮ for F♯ (sentence 45, and Ex. 3a). No theorist to my knowledge says more than that the ♭-*rotundum sive molle* must elicit the syllable fa. None says it entails fa of the soft hexachord. This negative evidence indicates only that the fa of the other hexachords is not excluded. Positive evidence is hard to come by, given the nature of the system, but the occurence of ♭ on F or C, fa in the natural and hard hexachords respectively, is well attested in the musical manuscripts. Similarly an A or E qualified by ♯ may belong to soft or natural hexachord. Thus, within the normal gamut we may have B♭ or A♮-♯ (soft hexachord), F♭ or E♮-♯ (natural) and C♭ or B♮-♯ (hard). For any of these pitches, qualified by these accidentals, to belong to other hexachords is possible only if the whole gamut is transposed, as shown in Table IV. To introduce transpositions of the system just to retain the association between soft hexachord and a ♭ on F or C would be to accept the more complex solution instead of the simpler one and must normally be disregarded: but it must remain open as a possibility for interpreting accidentals which cannot be made meaningful in any other way. For normal purposes, then, ♭ or ♮ does not commit the fa or mi to the soft or hard hexachord only.

24. Evidently in the manuscripts accidentals are used on pitches other than B, C, F (♭) and B, E, A (♮-♯). When used on any other pitches, the accidental makes the note fictitious, forming musica ficta as the theorists describe it. But if the recta accidental serves to indicate a recta hexachord, then for the same reasons the ficta accidental must relate to a fictitious or ficta hexachord. And if the correct syllables are to be sung, they and the pitches of the whole ficta hexachord ought to be inferred from the single accidental, and applied to any surrounding notes. In fact, to carry this theoretical possibility to its conclusion, a single accidental ought to imply not only the hexachord into which it fits, but also the whole system into which the hexachord fits as hard, soft, or natural. To know the place of the semitone is meaningful only within the context of the hexachord. Similarly, the hexachord must be related to a system of its own. By this extension a single ficta accidental showing the place of the semitone also implies a ficta gamut, a ficta system, or to put it more simply, a transposed system.

25. The proposition is not as extreme as it appears at first glance. We are quite accustomed, in eighteenth century theory, to the idea that a single accidental can change the whole system from one tonality to another, on a permanent or temporary basis. Moreover, the presence of a key-signature in medieval music can be explained successfully only in terms of a transposed hexachord system. The theorists do not refer to key-signatures, or to transposed systems (but compare Ugolino, 52-58): nor do they imply that notes other than those of the regular gamut can ever become recta. But they indicate quite clearly that musica recta is the norm for a piece of music. A consistently applied key-signature can 'deliver' a recta series of notes only in a transposed gamut. Furthermore, almost all the examples of musica ficta given by theorists involve the sharpening of notes and there are virtually no ficta flats to be found in the manuscripts themselves (55-56): one could infer that flats became associated with the recta of hexachords transposed by flat signatures, which are common. There exists no positive evidence for sharp signatures (37 & App. II): sharps therefore always remain unequivocally fictitious and thus form the principal ingredients for the theorists' descriptions of ficta.

The consequences of the hypothesis that flat signatures effect a transposition of the recta hexachords are:

a) the hexachords will be transposed flatwards as many degrees as there are different flats in the signature. For example, in a signature of B♭ & E♭ the hexachords will be on F, B♭ & E♭. As a result

b) the flat one degree farther than those of the signature becomes a recta note.[16a] Thus, in a signature of B♭ & E♭, the A♭ is recta and

c) the natural version of the pitches flattened by the signature become ficta notes, over which recta notes take precedence. Thus, in the B♭ & E♭ signature, B♮ and E♮ are ficta.

Further consequences could be postulated, and in certain circumstances modification of these results may be necessary, as in the case of a signature consisting of E♭ only (Old Hall No. 21).

26. The definition of recta and ficta according to the key-signature will affect what takes precedence in the choice of editorial accidentals, and let it be repeated once again, the theoretical preference is for recta (8).

From what has been said, it will appear that all sharps may be regarded as ficta. However, because we cannot, in our present state of knowledge, decide which of the three hexachords may be in use at a particular time, it is not possible to distinguish between recta and ficta flats. It is of course clear which *may* be recta, which *must* be ficta: in the B♭ & E♭ signature, an A♭ may or may not be recta depending on whether the soft hexachord could be in force, whereas a D♭ must be ficta.

The function of signatures as hexachord- rather than key-signatures may also apply to manuscript accidentals, thus giving every manuscript symbol of this sort the same meaning. For instance, in our B♭ & E♭ signature which allows a recta A♭, explicit manuscript placing of an A♭ may imply further flatward shifting of the system, giving the hexachord on A♭ with D♭ as recta.

27. Key-signatures, then, must be regarded as gamut or at least as hexachord signatures, indicating transposition. Although isolated manuscript accidentals may also have the same function their interpretation usually need not depend on such an extreme possibility. But the adding of editorial accidentals, which we incorrectly equate with musica ficta, has presented such problems to scholars, especially when the manuscript accidentals seem to

16a. This hidden implication of the signature--or even of an accidental within the stave (see section 48)--remained in theory and perhaps in practice at least until the early 17th century: Praetorius, in his *Syntagma Musicum III* (1619), p. 32, compares older usage with the practice he prefers. After a single B♭ (signature), E♭ is implied in older practice, where Praetorius marks the accidental.

It is worth noting that, because of its effect on the pitch E, the B♭ signature placed at the beginning of a stave may be justified even though no note of the pitch occurs on that stave. The same is true of an accidental B♭.

predetermine the situation, that any widening in the meaning of accidentals can only alleviate the difficulties. Before summarising the wider meanings of written accidentals, let us state more clearly what transpositions may be implied by each symbol. Table IV sets out the possibilities most frequently met with in the practical manuscripts: the logical extension for more extreme cases can easily be carried out by the reader. At the extreme left are shown the ♭ and ♮ relating only to the soft and hard hexachords respectively, in case the reader should feel they are best restricted in this way: the adjacent

TABLE IV

♭ in soft, ♮ in hard hex.	in others	Recta gamuts transposed						Solmization syllables
		a) normal gamut, untransposed	b) flatward transpositions		c) sharpward transpositions			
		dd	g	cc	aa	ee	bb	l-s
	♭	cc	f	bb♭	g	dd	aa	s-f
♮ ♭		bb (♮ / ♭)	e (♮ / ♭)	aa (♮ / ♭)	f (♯ / ♮)	cc (♯ / ♮)	gg (♯ / ♮)	m f
	♮	aa	d	g	e	bb	f♯	l-m-r
		g	c	f	d	aa	e	s- r-u
	♭	f	b♭	e♭	c	g	d	f-u
	♮	e	a	d	b	f♯	c♯	l-m
		d	G	c	a	e	b	l -s-r
	♭	c	F	b♭	G	d	a	s -f-u
♮ ♭		b (♮ / ♭)	E (♮ / ♭)	a (♮ / ♭)	F (♯ / ♮)	c (♯ / ♮)	G (♯ / ♮)	m f
	♮	a	D	G	E	b	F♯	l-m-r
		G	C	F	D	a	E	s-r -u
	♭	F	B♭	E♭	C	G	D	f-u
	♮	E	A	D	B	F♯	C♯	l-m
		D	Γ	C	A	E	B	s-r
	♭	C	F'	B♭	Γ	D	A	f-u
♮		B	E'	A	F♯'	C♯	Γ♯	m
		A	D'	Γ	E'	B	F♯'	r
		Γ	C'	F'	D'	A	E'	u

column shows them as they relate to the other hexachords. Alignment of the correct accidental symbol with the note-pitch before which it stands in the manuscript will indicate the transposition which may be implied. Thus, a manuscript C♮-♯ could theoretically imply the system built on E (natural hexachord) or the one on A (hard hexachord) or, extending the Table, the one on B (soft hexachord). The pitches noted in the Table are all recta for each transposition: any other pitch would be ficta.

The gamuts beginning on C and F, the flatward transpositions, would exist under the key-signatures of B♭ and B♭ & E♭ respectively or as a transitory 'modulation' after an accidental. In either case the note one degree further flatward than the signature or accidental would be flat by recta, i.e., the E♭ or A♭. We have already remarked that sharp signatures are unknown at this early period, and the sharpward transpositions must be assumed always to be transitory 'modulations' during the course of a piece, implied by an accidental.

28. I have stressed the invariable response of fa to ♭ and mi to ♮-♯: the Table shows conclusively that there are exceptions even to this rule. Under the key-signature of B♭ the soft hexachord, with E♭ as fa, begins with B♭, which must therefore be ut. Under the signature B♭ & E♭ the manuscript notes G-A-B♭ may need the recta A♭ supplied and the solmization would be mi-fa-sol, giving B♭-sol. Similarly in the sharpward transpositions ♮-♯ may have to be solmized with syllables other than mi: presumably any move this far away from the normal was avoided if at all possible because, as we can see, the basic principle of the system, that accidentals indicate the position of the semitone between mi and fa, is disappearing.

It is one thing to propose that transpositions of hexachord or gamut are shown by an accidental: it is another to use them constructively for analysis or for editorial addition. But the variety of meanings inherent in an accidental causes many of the features of manuscript chromaticism hitherto inexplicable, and provides the basis for many of the subsequent arguments. Before leaving Table IV it may be worth noting that even systems twice transposed have one hexachord in common with the untransposed system: even hexachords removed by four transpositions have five notes in common. These common notes may act as pivots through which transpositions may be linked.

29. The complexity of the system need not surprise us: it is no greater than that of the tonal system. And in the latter, a single accidental may be just as ambiguous, being either a temporary chromaticism or implying a real change of key, whether transitory or long-lasting. By means of hypothetical but logical extensions of the usual gamut, then, we may explain many features of the way manuscript accidentals are used. Nevertheless, the presence (or absence!) of unwritten accidentals in medieval music and the use of extemporisation to supply them must have forced the performers to keep to the simpler choices where possible; the simple alternative survived, and for practical purposes we should always consider it first. The following passage summarises the possible meanings of accidentals in order of likelihood. Alternative d) is merely one application of e), only a little more likely than e) itself. If e) is to be considered, the choice should begin with the most probable, e.g., ♭-fa in the soft and ♮-mi in the hard hexachord, then in other hexachords, followed by ♭ or ♮ relating to the other syllables (remembering that these are always implied normally when a key-signature occurs).

The possible meanings of accidentals are:

♭-fa a) lower the pitch by a semitone,
b) do not alter, if the note is already fa,
c) do not raise, e.g., cancelling a previous sharp,
d) the note below will be mi and may have to be sharpened if the flattened note cannot be lowered, with a corresponding adjustment of other notes within the hexachord range,
e) sing one of the transpositions shown in Table IV.

♮-♯-mi a) raise the pitch by a semitone,
b) do not alter, if the note is already mi,
c) do not lower, e.g., cancelling a previous flat,
d) the note above will be fa and may have to be flattened if the sharpened note cannot be raised,
e) sing one of the transpositions shown in Table IV.

These distinctions, as well as the recta/ficta difference, have to be borne in mind during any examination of manuscript accidentals, and during the following pages. Unless otherwise noted the simplest choice, that of a) and modern practice, is assumed to be in operation.

Key-signatures

30. In contrast with an unsignatured part, one with key-signature has extra chromaticism in recta notes and, by the simultaneous use of different signatures, the complete texture of a piece of music may be enriched with legitimate accidentals. By introducing, relative to the untransposed gamut, increased chromaticism in the form of recta flats, key-signatures eliminate the need for ficta sharps where these would otherwise be required to perfect or colour intervals. Perfection and colouration mostly require intervals to be expanded. Expansion by a flat can be achieved only by inflecting the lower note, and the application of a signature to the lowest voice is a convenient method of making available more recta flats than are present in an unsignatured part. But for those cadences which cannot be made Phrygian and for those imperfect intervals which cannot be corrected by flattening the lower note, sharps are necessary in the upper parts. To apply to those upper parts the same flat signature which renders recta flats in the lowest voice would make fictitious certain notes otherwise recta. Thus, the cadence $\genfrac{}{}{0pt}{}{\text{C-D}}{\text{E-D}}$ may be made correct without ficta alteration if the lower part has a signature of B♭ since the E♭ is recta:

$\left.\begin{array}{l}\text{no signature}\\ \text{signature }\flat\end{array}\right] \begin{array}{l}\text{C-D}\\ \text{E}\flat\text{-D.}\end{array}$ To give the upper part a similar flat signature would render the cadence to C incorrect: $\left.\begin{array}{l}\text{signature }\flat\\ \text{signature }\flat\end{array}\right] \begin{array}{l}\text{B}\flat\text{-C}\\ \text{D -C.}\end{array}$ D♭ is not a recta note under the signature of one flat and since ficta flats are not used (55-56) the correction $\genfrac{}{}{0pt}{}{\text{B}\flat\text{-C}}{\text{D}\flat\text{-C}}$ is not available. The only means of setting the cadence right is to introduce a ficta sharp on the B: $\left.\begin{array}{l}\text{sig. }\flat\\ \text{sig. }\flat\end{array}\right] \begin{array}{l}\text{B}\natural\text{-C}\\ \text{D -C.}\end{array}$ But the B♮ is ficta only because the upper voice has the signature. With different signatures in each part, both cadences are correct without the use of ficta notes:

$\left.\begin{array}{l}\text{sig. -}\\ \text{sig. }\flat\end{array}\right] \begin{array}{l}\text{C -D}\\ \text{E}\flat\text{-D}\end{array}$ and $\genfrac{}{}{0pt}{}{\text{B-C}}{\text{D-C.}}$

31. It is thus a typical practice of the period for lower voices to have additional flats in their signatures, a technique known and described under the terms 'partial...' or 'conflicting signatures' (see studies by Allaire, Apel, Hoppin and Lowinsky mentioned in the Bibliography). The reason for the technique, to my knowledge not previously offered, is simply the preservation of as much recta music as possible.

Signatures with both B♭ and E♭ begin to appear more frequently in the fifteenth century than earlier, presumably implying an increased use of the Phrygian cadence. This may relate to the more frequent use of the Phrygian mode which is sometimes noticeable in late fifteenth century works, as well as to the change in chromatic style which undoubtedly occurs at the same time.

32. With respect to the period of Old Hall, English descant pieces infrequently have a signature of any kind, but in the complex styles tenor and contratenor typically have the same signature of one flat more than the upper voices, Such an arrangement will be represented as –,b,b or b, eb, eb: that is, counting the upper voices as one unit and listing contratenor, then tenor. The abbreviation Beb shows the presence of both low and high B♭: the precise constitution of a composition's signature will always be given.

That the contratenor should also have more flats in its key-signature than the upper voices may be justified by its close association in name and range with the tenor. Functionally, it has to be treated like an upper voice, at least at cadences, although when it is lower in range than the tenor it may usurp the function of the voice: *and note that when the contratenor is lower than the tenor it is called tenor* (Coussemaker III, 466). And in fact, often as the contratenor has the same signature as the tenor, almost as often it has a different one. In this case the signature is usally the same as the upper voices': –,–,b. Rarely, it is different from both tenor and upper voices: b,eb,Beb (Nos 13 & 39, both by later scribes and composed by Damett) or b,e,eb (No. 21, Leonel). When the contratenor signature conflicts with the tenor's it may bespeak a certain difference in function: I discuss the relation between signature, style, and function in more detail in "Some Notes on the Early Fifteenth Century Contratenor" (*Music and Letters* L, 1969, p. 376), and in Appendix II.

33. When two flats are present in the signature the B♭ is sometimes but not always duplicated at the octave, apparently suggesting that signatures did not operate on all octave levels. The eb signature without duplication of the B♭ appears in the C_4 clef (as in No. 16, Roy Henry), in which the low B♭ is not obtainable in any case, but also sometimes in the C_5 or F clef in which it is available (as in No. 77, anon.). The low B♭ is the pitch omitted, if only one B♭ occurs in the signature: the arrangements eb and Beb are found, but never Be. The conclusion that signatures do not operate at all levels unless duplicated in both octaves should be discarded since the absence or presence of the low B♭ is probably dependent on the peculiar status of that pitch as a ficta note (8). Moreover, if signatures indicate transposition of the whole gamut, then automatically all octave levels are included.

Slight differences in signatures may simply reflect meaningless inconsistencies in the models from which the scribe worked although certain pieces suggest otherwise. In Nos 13 & 39 (paired movements by Damett but written down by different scribes of the later layers of the manuscript) the signatures are b,eb,Beb, although the clefs of tenor and contratenor are identical. In No. 39, a low B♭ signature has been erased from every line of the latter voice. The distinction must be meaningful: although we cannot provide a definite reason, it probably also lies in the ficta quality of the low B♭. However, since the tenor has the low B♭ while contratenor does not, a functional difference may also be involved.

The same difficulty with the low B♭ may account for the occasional really odd signature consisting of an E♭ only: No. 82 (anon.) has the scheme b,e,e (contratenor has an upper B♭ as an accidental for only the first stave): No. 21 (Leonel) differentiates tenor and contratenor — b,e,eb. Appendix II offers for such signatures an explanation for which there is at the moment little theoretical or musical evidence. Since the Bs at both octave levels usually need to be constantly flattened, whatever the signature, the simplest solution in transcription is to add editorial B♭ to the manuscript signature, a temporary compromise until further information is known.

Key-signature Cancellation

34. A signature pitch may be cancelled only by a ficta accidental. The note so cancelled remains recta and because of the restriction of ficta to places of absolute necessity a repetitition of the note, after its cancellation, ought to return to recta status whether or not the signature is restated. This appears to lead to the important principle that ficta accidentals of this kind serve only the note they affect, having a 'once-only' application; later notes of the pitch requiring obligatory ficta should probably receive it by extempore unwritten alteration rather than by presumptive continuation of the written accidental. Even if the cancellation of an accidental transposes the system, the same principle should probably apply. Thus, in a B♭ signature, B♮, a ficta accidental, may move the hexachords from recta C, F, B♭ to recta G, C, F, in which both B♭ and B♮ are recta, and a case could be argued for preserving the B♮ pitch beyond the immediately affected note. But the policy of calling on transposition only in extreme necessity would suggest that the new hexachords on G, C, F be treated as transitory ficta rather than transposed recta: even so, only the G hexachord is truly ficta, since the others are common with the C, F, B♭ set. In this case, then, the B♮ is truly ficta and the recta B♭ should be reinstated at once, if possible.

In Old Hall, signature accidentals are very rarely restated after cancellation: such a procedure would be totally unneccessary if the 'once-only' effect proposed were the accepted practice. Moreover, the notes between the cancellation and the next manuscript line mostly require the uncancelled, recta version of the pitch.

In the case of immediate repetition of the cancelled pitch, or of repetition within a recognisable ornamental figure, one may propose an exception to the 'once-only' rule or imagine the addition of unwritten accidentals. For the sake of relying on an unbreakable rule, the latter may be preferred.

35. In a signature of B♭ alone, the system-transposition possibly implied by the B♮ is clear: it becomes more complex in other signatures. In a B♭ & E♭ signature the hexachords are on F, B♭, E♭: E♮ may move them to C, F, B♭ with E♭ still a recta note, or directly to G, C, F in which E♭ is not available. We may prefer the closer transposition. But a subsequent B♮, or even a B♮ without a preceding E♮, would necessarily produce the farther transposition: thus, a B♮ alone would, if system-transposition is used, automatically cancel both B♭ and E♭ of the signature. Once again we have revealed a number of choices although we cannot yet say conclusively which is preferable and must rely on the assumption that the simpler is more likely.

36. There is an interesting adjunct: the omission of a signature at a new line may function in the same way as a natural sign within the line (but see the section on Latent Key-signatures). Two passages of several may be quoted. In No. 81 (Leonel) the B♭ signature on f.69, vii, is followed by stave viii with no signature. At this point the top voice is using G♯s, and B♮s are required in the tenor.

Ex. 4

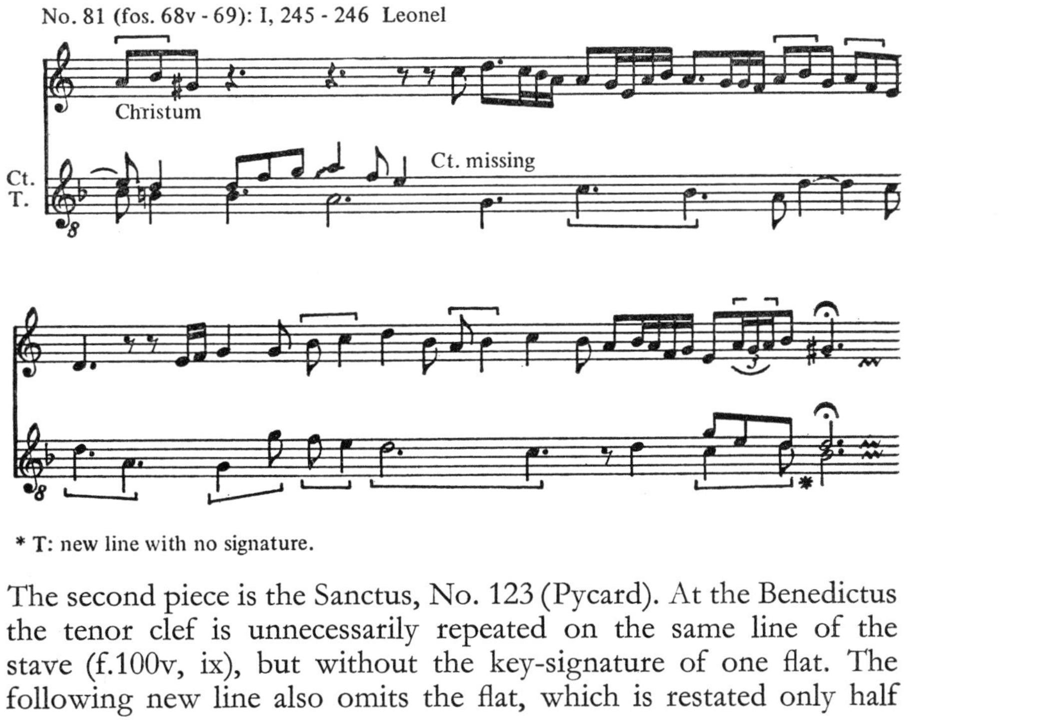

* T: new line with no signature.

The second piece is the Sanctus, No. 123 (Pycard). At the Benedictus the tenor clef is unnecessarily repeated on the same line of the stave (f.100v, ix), but without the key-signature of one flat. The following new line also omits the flat, which is restated only half way through that stave (OH I, 374-375). Such deliberate placing is unlikely to be the result of carelessness. At this point the Sanctus text is troped with the words *Mariae Filius*, which are often emphasised by fermatae or chromaticism. Moreover, the plainchant, in the upper canonic voices, at this place reaches for the only time its highest note, an E♮ which may need flattening by ficta, a highly unusual procedure (55-56), to avoid close harmonic proximity with the tenor B♭s, if they were present. Omission of the signature coincides with harmonic and textual necessity.

As in this piece, restatement of a clef without signature, and otherwise unnecessarily, may always cancel the latter, as it does in plainchant. In No. 28 (Pycard) the contratenor and alius contratenor are placed on the same stave as the tenor, but without clefs or signatures: here it seems likely that tenor clef and signature apply to all. On the other hand the contratenor of No. 76 (also Pycard) continues on the same stave as tenor, restating the same clef, but omitting the signature, which is absent for the remainder of the voice. The tenor of No. 79 (Bittering) presents conflicting evidence since it continues on the same stave as the contratenor, repeating the clef but not the signature, which is present on all subsequent staves. Is this a deliberate omission for only the very first notes of the tenor? If we assume careful, meaningful positioning of all symbols, we have to accept that such omissions probably signify something.

Intermittent Signatures

37. It is sometimes extremely difficult to be certain about the presence or absence of a signature. The tenor of No. 122 (Tyes) is based on a plainsong and has a number of statements of B♭ at new sections, quickly cancelled, quickly restated. Similarly, of the five staves of the contratenor three have B♭ signatures, but of the four new sections marked by manuscript bar-lines (other than at new staves) three have none. At times, when only one stave of several has a signature, and when close to the beginning of the line is a note to which that symbol could refer, we may be fairly sure that the symbol is simply an accidental fortuitously occuring at that point: one may quote No. 118 (Leonel), contratenor (f.97, x) and No. 82 (anon.), contratenor (f.70, xi). No. 95 (Typp) presents a different problem since at the beginning or close to the beginning of every new stave in the top voice is an F♯. We shall see that accidentals close to the beginning or end of a line may have been key-signatures at one stage in the transmission from manuscript to manuscript (see next section, Latent Key-signatures). But a signature of F♯ would be highly exceptional, if not unique, for the period[17]; it is inexplicable in terms of normal practice and cannot be accounted for as a transposed version of a normal signature arrangement. It is tempting to dismiss this as fortuitous occurence of accidentals near the beginning of four staves, but for one other disturbing feature: in the fourth stave and after a larger number of intervening notes than is usual for cancellation of a simple accidental there appears an f, for F♮ (OH I, 315, bar 29 F♯ — F♮ omitted in 35 as unnecessary in modern edition).

Latent Key-signatures[17a]

38. In the process of copying from manuscript to manuscript, the change of line in both the exemplar and copy demand a special care or initiative from the scribe because here there occur features, such as key-signatures, which are misplaced elsewhere. When the scribe sees, in his exemplar, a new line with a signature, he may be in the middle of a line in the copy: unless he is knowledgeable and careful, he may repeat the signature here. The modern editor is in a similar situation if, as in the cases just discussed, it is unclear whether or not accidentals at new lines are true signatures.

This may offer another explanation for the isolated manuscript line without signature, which I claimed may well be meaningful, or for those accidentals which are not followed by any applicable note, or for the unusually distant preplacing of some symbols (see section 41, Preplaced Accidentals).

Scribe A, the main scribe of Old Hall, is careful, knowledgeable, and may be presumed to manage his changes of line correctly. However, we cannot claim this care for the scribes of the exemplars which were before him: they may have erred at line changes, and scribe A may have identically copied their errors. Only with a specific exemplar and its direct copy could we be absolutely sure that line changes were responsible for oddities in signatures and accidentals. However, there are some interesting pieces in Old Hall which it may be well to examine a little further.

39. The length of manuscript lines and the amount of music they hold does not vary greatly from one source to another of

17. For a 13th century secular song which appears to have such a signature see Jean Beck, "Les Chansonniers des Troubadours et Trouvères", vol. I, *Le Chansonnier Cangé*, facs. ed., Philadelphia 1927, fol. 103v. Compare also British Museum, Add. MS 36929, f.59.

17a. Cf. Lowinsky "The Function. . ." p. 240

comparable dimensions: thus, at the beginning of a piece at least, the new line is likely to occur within a few notes of the exemplar's change of line. Signatures incorrectly transferred would appear near the beginnings and ends of lines in the copy rather than at the correct place. There are one or two Old Hall pieces in which just such a placing of accidentals may be observed. Consider the top voice of No. 145 (Bittering). There are certain points here where the hypothesis breaks down, as in stave iii, but quite consistently a B♭ appears near the beginning or end of staves, and where it does not appear one could make out a case for deliberate omission as the music approaches a cadence on C (as at the word *indolis*, OH I, 416, bars 30-31), requiring B♮. However, in this composition the B♭s are all immediately before or very near the note B and may thus be true accidentals. But there remains no doubt that the voice would have been simpler (for the modern editor at least) if a B♭ signature had been used.

In No. 8 (Aleyn), on the first two staves of the lowest part, there is no signature. A B♭ appears nine notes after the beginning of stave iii, at a new section: another appears nine notes into stave iv, a third eleven notes into stave v, a fourth at the beginning of stave vi. None of these is immediately before the note B. We may be right in suspecting a hidden key-signature, and this possibility has to be remembered when applying editorial accidentals, although of course no definite conclusion can be stated without a great deal more evidence. I discuss this piece in detail in Appendix I.

Position of Accidentals

40. It is our convention to place accidentals immediately before the note they affect: such was not always the case in music of early times. Apart from slight vertical misplacing of the symbols too high or low, a feature which is occasionally to be found in Old Hall (e.g., No. 75, anon., *in celum* — B♭ too low, perhaps an A♭ too high), there are three horizontal positions which have to be mentioned: a) immediately before the note affected or before the ligature of which that note forms a part, b) directly above or below a note, c) preplaced and followed by intervening notes or symbols.

Of these, a) needs no further discussion. Occasionally the accidental is difficult to handle or even inexplicable, but these features cannot be related to its position. We may deal with b) briefly. It may be a chance result of placing the notes so close together that the symbol falls directly above or below another note before the one it affects: this may be so whether the symbol is directly before or, as in c), preplaced. As far as can be ascertained, in Old Hall these are the only possibilities for b), both of which are insignificant. However, in a number of sources, including especially the Paduan concordance with Old Hall No. 33 (Zacar), the accidental frequently is placed below or above the note it is intended to affect, and not before it (see Plate I). Rare occurences of this are to be found in some English sources, but none occurs unmistakably in Old Hall. Such positioning of accidentals may simply be a matter of space and all such occurences may be the result of later addition and have no other significance.

As for c), the situation is very complex:

Preplaced Accidentals

41. Preplacing accidentals is a common feature of all manuscripts of the Middle Ages and early Renaissance, including plainchant sources. In Old Hall nearly half the total number of accidentals do not immediately precede the relevant note, but stand some distance before it. More facts about the precise usage of Old Hall will be shown in the following pages. Common though it is, no theorist describes the practice. Prosdocimus says

> that when these signs [♭ & ♮] are placed in order to colour a certain consonance, they ought always to be placed immediately before the note whose syllable [*or* pitch] (*vox*) has to be changed in order to colour such a consonance, whether that note be in the tenor or discant, and whether it be on a line or in a space, since whatever the sign, it does not serve properly except for the note immediately following. (Coussemaker III, 198).

If *vox* means pitch, as it may, then Prosdocimus would allow only the procedure we use nowadays, ignoring the frequent practice of contemporary sources, of which he may in fact disapprove. More likely is that *vox* here means solmization syllable, also a standard usage of the word. The implications of this latter translation will be considered in turn. Let us first discuss a few simple reasons why accidentals might occur earlier than is necessary.

42. A scribe may have remedied an omission, or a later user may have made an addition, in the nearest available space before a note. But we may discount omission and replacement as a serious factor in a careful manuscript, the more so because there are sufficient examples of preplacing where space is available immediately before a note, or at least closer to it (e.g., OH f.28v, vi; 20v, vii — two instances; 74v, vi). There are, too, some instances of erasure and repositioning, sometimes farther from, sometimes closer to, the note (e.g., OH f.4, vii; 39, vii; 81v, viii). Even though in these cases the accidentals may have been erroneously written twice and one erased rather than a single symbol repositioned (Bent, diss., 107), there are sufficient indications that the exact position of the symbol had some meaning. Yet another moderately simple reason stems from the incorrect transference of key-signatures, previously discussed (38): if transferred incorrectly, a key-signature, bearing no spatial relationship to one particular note, may occur as an isolated symbol which appears like a preplaced accidental. This explanation applies only to accidentals which are acceptable as key-signatures, that is, almost exclusively B♭s.

Omission, later addition and incorrect signatures provide fortuitous rather than purposive reasons. One factor which requires accidentals necessarily to be preplaced stems from the nature of the solmizing system.

43. Although we do not know fully how to solmize polyphonic parts from this period, it is certain that the change from one hexachord to another, called mutation and necessitating a note common to both old and new hexachords, cannot take place on mi or fa when these represent different inflections of the same pitch, as with B♭-fa/B♮-mi. The mutation therefore cannot occur on the inflected pitch, since this is the precise meaning of the accidental. If hexachord change is to take place it must anticipate the inflected note, and the symbol denoting the new hexachord, i.e., the accidental, must be placed earlier than the pitch to which it refers.

If the accidental is to serve as a hexachord signature it must necessarily be preplaced. A logical consequence is that where an accidental stands immediately before its note, no mutation takes place.

That preplaced accidentals indicate mutation of the whole hexachord receives some support from the statement of Prosdocimus previously quoted. Reading solmization syllable for *vox* would give the following translation: *[accidentals] ought always to be placed immediately before the note whose syllable has to be changed.* Changing the syllable entails changing the hexachord to the one which includes the inflected note.

Although this hypothesis is logical and simple, and in the practical sources shows some promise of success, it is not the only reasonable solution which can be offered. The following paragraphs investigate the exact procedures in Old Hall, relating them chiefly to the mutation theory but also elucidating other reasons which may account for the phenomenon.

44. Any accidental, whether recta or ficta, whether cancelling a previous accidental or restating a signature, regardless of the specific symbol, may be placed early. Only one statistical result appears significant: the number of preplaced accidentals, nearly half the total number, is much higher in key-signatures of b,eb,eb or b,Beb,Beb. This may be because the signature implies a hexachord system already twice transposed from normal, and consequently the mutation or transposition points may be obscure enough to need more careful indication in the form of written, and preplaced, accidentals.

The symbol is often separated from the note to which it applies by only a single rest. This can have nothing to do with mutation, which requires the intervention of a solmizable note. Another reason, which may also apply when notes intervene, is easily found. Being of secondary importance, a *color*, an ornament, compared to the notes and rests, the accidental must not interfere with the meaning of the other symbols (68). In mensural notation the grouping of notes and of notes and rests is often of primary importance. The accidental is placed early so that, for example, two minim rests and a minim note will form a single group immediately obvious to the eye. There can be little doubt that the necessities of mensural grouping cause some preplacements: many occur in *prolatio major* or *tempus perfectum* where the grouping of perfections is specially important so that alteration and imperfection may be clear. In other words, the accidental sometimes functions as a *punctus divisionis* (84).

This kind of preplacing nearly always involves only one or two intervening symbols; i.e., the accidental comes early by the amount of the perfection preceding the note. Thus we get situations such as the following (in the next few examples, the exact spacing must be compared with the manuscript original):

Ex. 5

No. 118(f. 97, vi) Leonel — No. 36 (f. 30v, v) Cooke — No. 79 (f.66 v, vi) Bittering

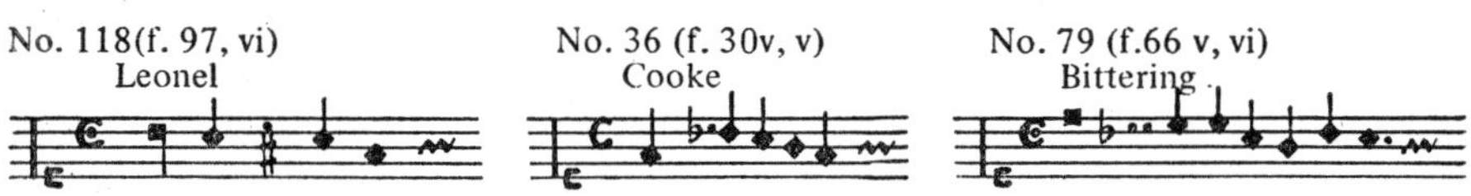

Occasionally in a complicated context mensural grouping may necessitate a longer distance between accidental and note, as in this passage involving imperfection *a parte ante*:

Ex. 6

No. 33 (f. 28v, xi) Zacar

Separation of the E from the previous D by the flat could easily have obscured the rhythm.

Careful grouping of notes and rests may also be required to indicate correct textual underlay, as in some passages of Old Hall music (Bent, diss., 110f.) This, too, could be a reason for preplacing accidentals, although no Old Hall examples can be quoted. Accidentals placed in particular positions to clarify note-grouping need have no special function in solmizing and do not relate to the mutation theory.

45. The number of symbols (counting ligatures as one symbol) between accidental and note is usually small, one note or rest, or two or three notes being quite the most common. Strict English descant style seems to have a higher proportion of longer interventions, and the simpler nature of the style could account for this. However, for the moment descant will be separated from the complex styles.

Complex styles. In these one point emerges immediately: about two thirds of the passages with more than three intervening symbols occur in works by Leonel, including a few in works which have quite reasonably been ascribed to him, even though strictly anonymous in the sources. Accidentals may thus provide an additional piece of evidence for attribution of anonymous pieces. Of the remaining one third, one passage is by an unnamed composer and Cooke, Bittering, Typp and Pycard are responsible for the others. In fact, of those passages by known composers with only three intervening notes, half are by Leonel (including two passages probably by him). A few others are anonymous. Most of the passages with three or more intervening symbols are to be found in Nos 84, 81 and 25 (all by Leonel), which are elsewhere singled out because of their exceptional chromatiscism.

Descant. Of the English descant pieces Nos 8 (Aleyn) and 61 (Chirbury) contain an unusual number of long intervening passages. Aleyn, Chirbury and Typp are responsible for most of these, whereas Leonel is responsible for one passage only of his eight descant pieces. The insular style thus receives somewhat unusual treatment from three composers who are known only in England whereas Leonel, known chiefly from continental sources, avoids this particular unusual feature even though he uses it considerably in the complex works. May we deduce from this that there was a different significance to preplaced accidentals dependent on the style? Or is it simply a question of what was familiar to the composer? Insular composers use distantly preplaced accidentals in descant, avoid them in the imported styles; the one composer known chiefly from continental manuscripts avoids them in descant, even though writing a number of such pieces, but employs them frequently elsewhere.

Here are the longest intervening passages in both styles:

Ex. 7

No. 103 (f. 85v): I, 332
Anon. (descant)

No. 77 (f. 65): I, 222
Anon. (chanson)

No. 7 (f. 5): I, 15 - 16
Cooke (chanson)

* new line, with bar, in MS.

The flat of the third example may be a key-signature, being repeated at the beginning of the next manuscript line, although not at other new lines.

46. How do intervening notes work with the mutation theory? In order for that theory to be good it seems necessary that all intervening notes fit the hexachord implied by the accidental. This is not invariably so, although it is most often the case. But it is in fact of no concern. I have already discussed the assumption that accidentals may imply transposition of the whole system as well as mutation. Thus, even if the intervening range exceeds the one hexachord, there may be the possibility of temporary mutation to another hexachord within the same transposition. In more than two thirds of the passages the range is within the hexachord implied by the accidental. However, if the upper or lower semitones (occasionally sharp or flat by alteration) are accepted as illegitimate extensions of the single hexachord, about four fifths of the intervening passages work. Such extensions of the hexachords without mutation may just have been used, even though they represent a perversion of the system. If they were solmized at all, they would probably have taken the syllables indicating the bottom and top of a semitone: la fa la for A B♭ A etc., ut mi ut for G F♯ G etc. Some theoretical evidence exists for the first of these[18]. The figures are probably conservative, since of the remaining fifth less than half

18. The unfortunate ditty *una nota super la semper est canendum fa* is not documentable from medieval sources and is surely the product of a quite different attitude. The earliest version I know, drawn to my attention by Zenoby Lawryshyn, is in Praetorius' *Syntagma Musicum III* (1619), p. 31: *unica notula ascendente super la, semper canendum esse fa*. Constant quotation of

quite definitely will not work and the rest are passages a) whose solmization is unclear because we do not know what syllable a symbol such as f implies, or b) about which there is some other insoluble problem.

Of the small proportion of intervening passages which will not work in the same hexachord — say at most one out of twelve — no explanation can be given for the majority. They occur more often after preplaced C♯ or G♯ than after F♯, even though the total number of C♯s and G♯s combined is far less than the number of F♯s written into Old Hall. Perhaps the farther removed from the normal the chromaticism was, with a greater likelihood of ♯ representing a syllable other than mi (28), the more difficult it became to keep track of what was within the implied hexachord. With almost no exceptions preplaced C♯s and G♯s are not required for the obligatory completion of a vertical perfection, and may be omitted without causing harmonic difficulty (No. 75, anon., is a good example; see OH I, 201), although many are used to sharpen the third or sixth before fifth or octave. Whether these features are significant or are related to the specific point in question it is not possible to say.

47. A few of the unsolmizable intervening passages have the accidental placed near a large leap which can be solmized neither in the new hexachord nor within the one in force and since there is no pitch common to both hexachords normal mutation is impossible. In these cases, and also when they are not preplaced, such accidentals may function as guides to abnormal solmization or indications of pitch. Thus, if a note near which an accidental physically stands is very distant, in terms of solmizing, from the hexachord of the accidental, that may sometimes be the very reason for the preplacing, the symbol serving instead of the note common to two hexachords upon which mutation would normally occur. An early warning of large shifts of tessitura may have been useful:

Ex. 8

No. 82 (f. 70, ii): I, 253
Anon.

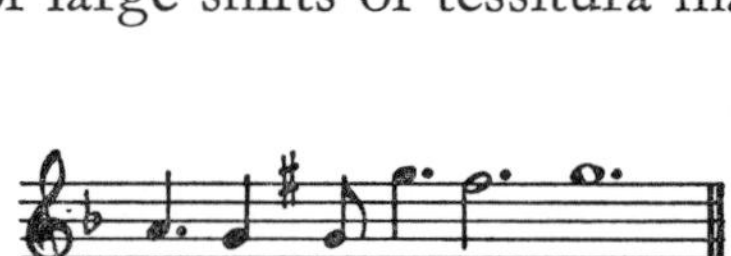

(cont. on following page)

this couplet perpetuates the perversion of incorrect solmizing, as well as our own rigidity because of the *semper*. La fa la is not within normal usage. Nevertheless, irregular solmizing was certainly known in the Middle Ages: see Coussemaker II, 293; IV, 223a ...*aut improprie sumere*; and especially IV, 376-380 where the second stave of the musical example on 380, if the print is to be trusted, shows precisely A-la B♭-fa A-la instead of A-la-mi B♭-fa A-mi-la.

Ex. 8 cont.

No. 82 (f. 70, iv): I, 258
Anon.

* in error for G.

No. 23 (f. 19, i): I, 49
Leonel

For this function it is not necessary for any subsequent note of the relevant pitch to follow the accidental. Such an instance is shown in Ex. 50.

Although the analytical tool is still too blunt to be of detailed value, there appears to be no limitation to the pitch of the note near which the preplaced symbol is written: when mensural preplacing does not offer an explanation, and if the indication of mutation or transposition is the only reason apparent, the note where the change has to be made does not appear to be restricted either to a pitch or to a particular syllable.

48. We have seen a glimmering of the reasons for preplacing: in mensural or pitch-giving cases it is clear. For mutation or transposition, however, we have so far explained again only the function of accidentals, not the reason for preplacing by a specific distance, four notes rather than three, or seven rather than two. This leads us to the question: why may it have been necessary to indicate a precise point of mutation or transposition? Preplacing itself derives partly from the rule forbidding mutation on mi or fa when representing the inflected note: the exact place of writing the symbol may have been important if the intervening music was changed thereby. The two ways in which such a change could occur are as follows:

Firstly, the accidental may entail other unwritten accidentals. For example, a B♭ before a passage in which Es occur may call for the flattening of those Es by making both E♭ and E♮ accessible as recta notes (see footnote 16a): a C♯ may call for sharpening of an F as la in the hexachord on A. Several instances of the principle as it applies to sharps are shown here:

Ex. 9

No. 29 (fos. 24v - 25): I, 90
Rowlard

No. 81 (fos. 68v - 69): I, 247 Leonel

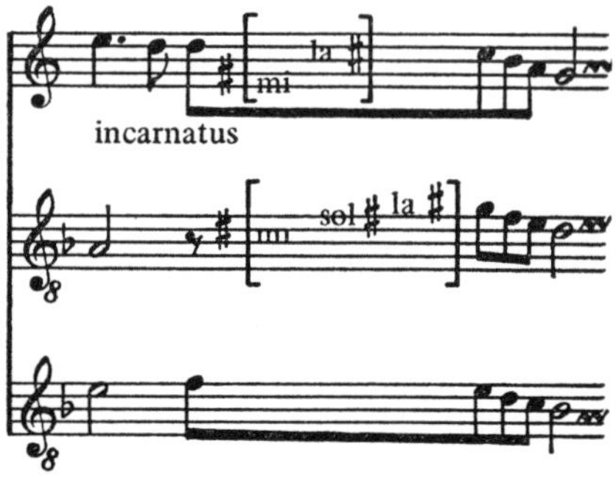

On the other hand if both accidentals are correct and correctly positioned F♯ cannot be employed for the upper voice in this passage:

Ex. 10

No. 84 (fos. 71v - 72)
I, 267 Leonel

This principle can apply only to the farther sharps, which imply the nearer ones, F♯ itself implying a B♮ which is already available —and to flats, each flat introducing the flat one degree more extreme. If we assume this function to be correct a preplaced B♭ ought to imply obligatory flattening of subsequent Es, since preplacing the ♭ has a meaning only if this *is* the function. This is evidently impossible in many cases:

Ex. 11

No. 25 (fos. 20v - 21): I, 61 Leonel

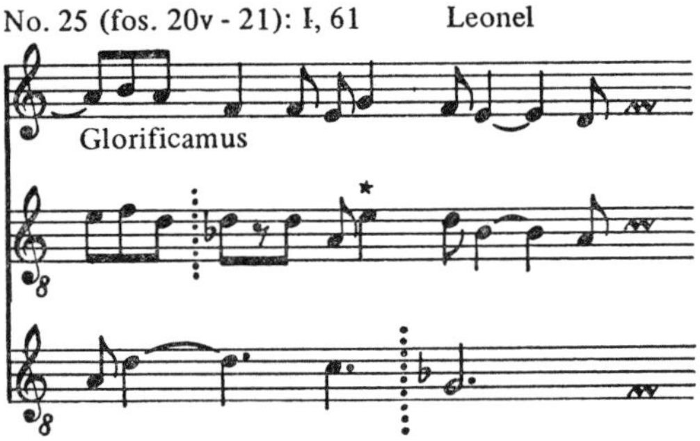

The new staves marked with dotted lines here have preplaced flats which in both cases are probably accidentals, not key-signatures: the E marked with an asterisk could just be flattened (see sections 69-72 for reference to imperfect melodic intervals), but would probably be better left natural. Thus, a ficta accidental may imply alteration of notes less distant, a recta one alteration of pitches farther distant.

49. Secondly, rather than to imply them, preplacing may be to prevent unwritten accidentals. This is a much more likely function, and seems to be justified in many instances:

Ex. 12

No. 116 (f. 94v - 95): I, 352 Leonel

Here the preplaced flat for fa makes the F ut: it therefore cannot be mi and sharp. The impending cadence on G would have made sharpening, at least of the second F, almost obligatory by melodic rules: similarly the expansion of the third to a fifth at the first F would raise the possibility of F♯. Both of these Fs, the second not directly, have been prevented from alteration. If we accept the natural quality of the second F as a consequence of the hexachord implied, this may go some way to confirming the correctness of the lower voice, whose C, causing a bare fourth with the F, may be suspect. An augmented fourth would be much more so.

A similar but more complex passage occurs here:

Ex. 13

No. 25 (fos. 20v - 21): I, 60 - 61 Leonel

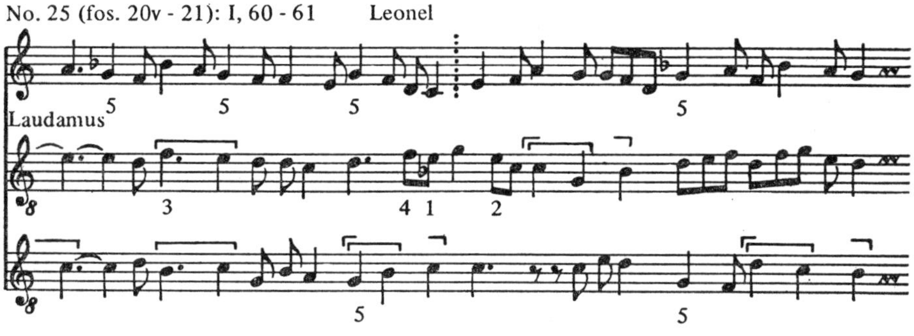

The B♭ of the middle voice (a black sign applying to a red context) could cause acceptable flattening of the E (1), but not of the E (2) unless the E of the top voice were flattened by aural analogy: the B♭ is not preplaced for mensural reasons, there being space for it nearer the note it affects without disturbing the grouping; it is not placed by a large melodic leap as an aid to correct pitch-solmizing. It is clearly placed under an F (4) although there is adequate space at other points. An F♯ has occured much earlier in the line, and the D, G, C hexachord group, allowing F♮ for the F (3), could still be in force, also allowing F♯ for F (4), which would be reasonable melodically. The preplaced B♭ might be to prevent such sharpening. The preplaced flats in the top voice, separated by a new stave as shown, may be explained mensurally, as well as by the necessity to clarify whether the F or the B is to be altered.

50. Many preplaced F♯s or B♭s seem to be associated with passages in which both notes occur. As in the two contexts of the previous example, melodically it may be reasonable to sharpen the F rather than flatten the B: indeed the Gs (5) prominently at the beginning of perfections may have implications of the hard hexachord with B♮ and perhaps a subsemitone. Preplacing the flat clarifies the 'colour' of the F: preplacing an F♯ may clarify the 'colour' of a B.

However, as in the above two places of the upper voice, the sign is placed still earlier than necessary: if the sole purpose here is to clarify the F, the accidental could precede it rather than the note before. We may see two reasons complementing each other. To clarify the F, the accidental must precede it; but in order not to obscure the mensural grouping it cannot stand immediately before and has to be preplaced even earlier.

51. There may be other reasons for preplacing, and certainly all the information is not yet available. However, we may summarise the tentative conclusions reached so far. Accidentals are preplaced

i) to clarify (or to avoid obscuring) note-grouping, for mensural or textual purposes,

ii) to indicate that mutation, which cannot take place where the accidental stands immediately before its note, must be employed,

iii) to indicate the point of hexachord mutation or system-transposition so that a) chromatic alteration which might otherwise be applied is not available, b) alteration which would not otherwise have been made is available. In this case, alterations both of whose alternatives are recta notes (e.g., E♮ or E♭ after B♭) retain their ambiguity and the alteration is optional, whereas in the cases in which one alternative is ficta, the other recta, there may be no choice (e.g., F♮s after a C♯ are ficta according to the hexachords in force, and F♯s as the recta alternative may be obligatory),

iv) to indicate the pitch or solmization syllable where one or the other might be obscure by reason of a large leap.

Accidentals are also preplaced because of

v) a shift, during copying, of an original new stave and signature so that the latter now occurs in the body of rather than at the beginning of the line,

vi) simple correction or addition in the nearest available preceding space.

Each case may combine any or perhaps all of these reasons, and has to be examined in its own context.

Retrospective effect

52. It seems unthinkable that a symbol may have an effect before its visual appearance. But this is the case even with music from eras familiar to us: the figure denoting proportions such as septuplets, conventionally placed in the middle, has an effect from the beginning of the phrase, perhaps two inches earlier (Chopin, Nocturne, Op. 9, No. 1, third complete bar); the whole bar rest, and in the nineteenth century often the whole bar note, appears in the middle of the bar. Performers do not sing from isolated notes: they take in phrases. Medieval performers were able to assimilate at a glance much longer phrases than is possible with modern notation (90), and that accidentals may have an effect before their physical appearance should not be difficult to believe. Until fresh information is available the editor needs to invoke the retrospective principle to explain only one situation in medieval music: occasionally a reiterated pitch is separated by an accidental. An instance appears in Ex. 20: two others are on stave x of Old Hall folio 82v (OH I, 321, bars 18-20, omits the second instance as unnecessary in modern edition).

Placing the symbol in such a position may be a means of circumventing the 'once-only' principle for accidentals which the following section elucidates.

Continuation of Effect

53. Of the large number of accidentals, only a very small proportion is cancelled. If the pitch should recur before a cancellation generally to continue the effect of the accidental is impossible: sometimes the continuation will cause no difficulty, sometimes it is needed to perfect an interval or sharpen a third or sixth, but the occasions on which the accidental may continue are exceeded by those in which it definitely will not work.

Statistics from a large number of sources would, I suspect, confirm these results drawn from Old Hall, placing the weight of evidence somewhat in favour of a 'once-only' rule but balanced by instances in which the effect may be continued. The number of the latter would be too large for them to be regarded as isolated exceptions, a fact apparently negating the 'once-only' principle. This statistical dilemma has resulted in our failure to resolve the problem of how long accidentals are valid.

But the logic of the statistics is false: when an accidental appears to continue in effect, each subsequent need for it may be met not by continuing the written symbol, but by an extempore addition quite unrelated to the latter and applied as though it had not occurred. The written symbol in these circumstances retains a 'once-only' effect.

54. In any case, the 'once-only' principle is clearly implied for ficta accidentals, since recta must be preferred except where ficta is needed or specified. For recta accidentals themselves both versions of the inflected note are equally available after the written symbol, but the 'once-only' principle may still be applied:

Ex. 14

No. 25 (f. 20v, vi - vii): I, 63 Leonel

The fourth B of the example (and perhaps also other notes) must be altered by musicianship, or by rule, as a cadence point. We also have to bear in mind that the second accidental may have a different significance unrelated to that of the first.

A convention requiring a 'once-only' application need not surprise us: Prosdocimus' statement that *[the accidental] does not serve properly except for the note immediately following* (41) seems to imply such a principle. In the absence of a theoretical or musical guide to any other policy, such a procedure is the only safe one for the modern editor to adopt. One may compare the identical usage in contemporary scores. Finally, it may be noted that to assume that an accidental may continue in effect has no rational basis whatsoever. Only the arbitrary and non-musical convention of the nineteenth century, in which a symbol remains in force until cancelled by a natural or by a barline, could have suggested such a procedure for earlier music.

55. Is the 'once-only' principle valid if the accidental implies transposition of system or hexachord? An F♯-mi causes a shift of the normal hexachords on G, C, F to those on D, G, C, and the ♭-fa, ♮-mi which applies to B in the recta scheme now applies to F, which may thus be either sharp or natural within the transposition. The principle is still valid and holds good for all transpositions by sharps. On the other hand transposition by means of a recta accidental does not have the same result: a B♭ implies shifting the G, C, F hexachords to C, F, B♭ giving E♭ and E♮ as the variable pitch. The B♭ itself, however, remains firmly flat. As an acceptable key-signature the B♭, if treated as a signature, entails its own continued effect. In this fact may lie the acceptance of flat and rejection of sharp key-signatures. The editor here has a choice, usually with no evidence for one solution or the other, of accepting B♭ as an accidental with B♮ still recta, or as a signature with B♮ a ficta pitch.

Two clues exist. The need for ficta notes after an accidental may help to determine its status: if by treating it as a signature (implying prolonged validity for its system and hexachords) more ficta notes are required than would be necessary if it were a simple accidental, then the latter interpretation should be preferred. Secondly, as far as can be ascertained from a perusal of numerous medieval sources, flats on further degrees must be preceded by nearer ones which make them recta, and arise only if the latter imply system-transposition. To put it more simply, and as a principle subject to further statistical confirmation: ficta flats are not normally written into medieval manuscripts. 'Ficta flat' appears to be a contradiction in terms. Thus, E♭s are not written in unless preceded by a B♭ or in a B♭ signature, A♭s occur only after E♭s (after B♭s) or in a B♭ & E♭ signature:

Ex. 15

Logically then, in the following hypothetical example the B♭, to produce the E♭, must be treated as a signature, entailing flats on all the Bs, and not as an accidental after which the other Bs could be natural:

Ex. 16

56. In Old Hall, and of course in other sources, there are some oddities: a few ficta flats in No. 76 (Pycard) are explicable by the extraordinary circumstances of the double clefs in that piece (see the notes in OH III). An E♭ without preceding B♭ of any kind occurs at the opening of No. 82 (anon.), but this is a key-signature in itself, being repeated at every new line. Another E♭ in the Amen of the upper voice of No. 83 (Leonel) occurs in the only line in the piece without B♭ signature: it would be reasonable to suppose error of some kind here. Only in No. 116 (Leonel) are there two E♭s not preceded by B♭s.

We may thus state another most important principle which has guided the editorial alteration in Old Hall: normally no flats should be introduced which are not available as recta.

One interesting passage may be noted:

Ex. 17

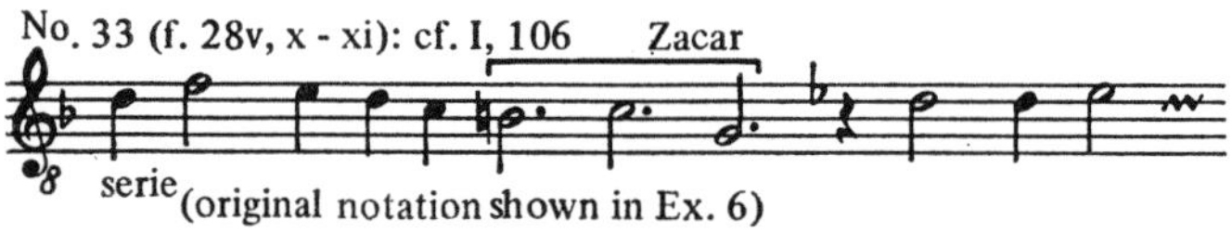

The 'once-only' effect of the ficta B♮ will leave the B♭ signature still in force, allowing E♭ to be recta.

57. To summarise: accidentals *per se* affect only the note they precede. Ficta sharps imply a system-transposition in which the sharp may apply later or not; flats may or may not imply a transposition, as necessary; 'ficta' flats always entail the continued effect of a preceding recta flat. The hexachords implied by transposition, if assumed, may remain in force until cancelled in some way. Assumption of the preceding principles allows us to explain those features which seem to belie the 'once-only' application of accidentals. For example, a small proportion of manuscript accidentals are cancelled, a fact which has previously led to the unworkable supposition that their effect was continuous. It is now clear that 'cancelling' may be either a) related to and negating a previous accidental, the simplest role, or b) an independent phenomenon unrelated to a preceding accidental, or c) a cancelling of a whole transposition. Another question now arises: why was transposition cancelled in only a small number of cases? The answer lies partly in the fact that a one degree transposition still retains two hexachords in common with the untransposed system, and those two hexachords in all their octave duplications were probably sufficient for very lengthy passages of music. Even a two degree transposition would have one complete hexachord in common with the untransposed system, and of the eight notes of that system only two would be unavailable.

Moreover, the transposition may be changed not only by cancelling the specific symbol which caused it, but also by placing any other accidental. Thus, a C♯ would call for hexachords on A, D, G; a subsequent F♯ for those on G, D, C, automatically cancelling the C♯. In addition, if it has a signature change, a new line in the manuscript (or, occurring at unknown different positions, in its exemplars) or a new section may effect a cancellation by implying a return to the recta hexachords. So too, may an unnecessary change in clef, which is a regular means of cancelling a B♭ signature sometimes found in plainsong.

Cancelling symbols

58. In this section I refer to the cancelling of an accidental or key-signature by a 'natural' of the same specific pitch, assuming a relation between the two, and to the restoration of recta or untransposed system by reiterating the signature or deliberately negating a previous ficta accidental. Because of the key-signature/ accidental ambiguity in certain cases, it is extremely difficult to see a meaningful distinction between a flat signature with natural ficta, and no signature with flat recta. An editor needs to examine both possibilities.

Mi is cancelled in two ways: F♯ is sometimes negated by ♭-fa, more often by the sign f (the York concordance with Old Hall employs the letter c, surely an error). C♯ and G♯ are similarly affected by c and g. The few D♯s are not cancelled in Old Hall. Logically, all mi signs should be rectified by ♭-fa and we should ask why this is not used for C or G and only on occasion for F. Probably the answer lies in the fact that ♭ means fa, whereas f, c, g may not. We have no information as to what syllables these may imply although the most obvious supposition is that they signify ut, representing the beginning of the three recta hexachords on G, C, F. In the following example ut seems more probable for the F, but if so why is the ♭ necessary since the B would automatically be fa?

Ex. 18

No. 143 (f. 109v, vi): I, 408 Anon

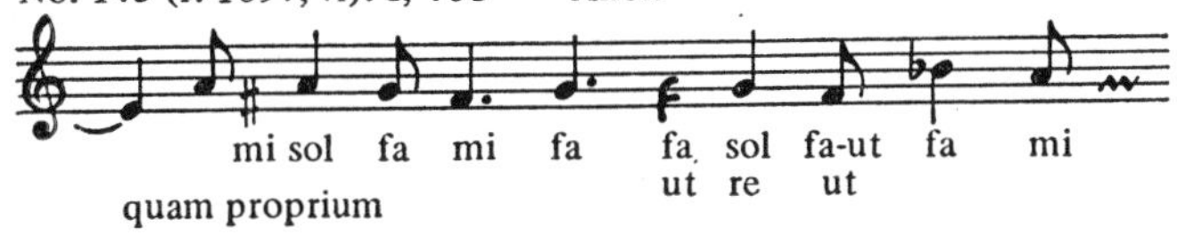

The cancelling of F♯ by ♭ or f may be because the pitch F can, by musica recta, be either ut or fa, whereas the cancelling of G by ♭ would make it fa in a ficta hexachord. On the other hand, C may also be ut or fa by musica recta, and its ♯ too could logically be cancelled by ♭: it never is. There can be no question but that solmization sometimes becomes extremely complex in the face of accidentals and cancellers:

Ex. 19

No. 83 (f. 70v, iii): I, 259 - 260 Leonel

Here an E♯ apparently cancels the previous E♭ as well as F♯, by making the semitone occur above E. Since the second F is thus already fa the following symbol f is superfluous if it signifies fa. But since the melodic line descends after that symbol it is also meaningless as ut. In fact, the F♯, by changing the hexachord, has already achieved the cancelling of the E♭, thus rendering E♮ superfluous except to cancel the F♯. Unless some at present unknown function resides in accidentals, solmization breaks down in passages like this and the symbols cannot be related to each other. Such situations may result from the superimposition of different incompatible layers of accidentals: if this circumstance is proven, some of the written-in accidentals are invalid and will have to be ignored.

59. Where an accidental is cancelled certain general rules can be ascertained: a) the cancelling symbol is invariably on the same manuscript stave, suggesting a relation between it and its accidental. No exceptions to this have been noted in Old Hall. This is further evidence that the ends of manuscript lines are of some importance for limiting the continued effect of an implied transposition. Cancelling by this means must have been extremely hazardous in view of the difficulties caused by copying (38); b) cancellers often appear long before the next note of the relevant pitch. The number of notes between is an average of six, ranging from one to ten: anything greater than this tends to be unusual. There are nearly twenty cancellers with notes of the relevant pitch between them and their accidentals; sometimes the same inflection must be re-introduced to correct harmonic situations or for aesthetic reasons (Nos 75, anon.; 89, Pennard; 122, Tyes; 51, Fonteyns; 61 & 132, Chirbury; 81 & 96, Leonel; 98 & 106, Typp). When notes and a further accidental come between the accidental and its canceller the two may be unrelated:

Ex. 20

Not necessarily redundant, the B♯ may not relate to the B♭. In the hexachord implied by the F♯ the upper B is natural, being la, which the B♯ changes to mi.

60. Really difficult passages occur in several pieces (Nos 36, Cooke; 50, Bittering; 52, Cooke; 83 & 84, Leonel; 95, Typp). Nos 36 and 84 have many accidentals inexplicable and difficult to handle. In the other four pieces we may perhaps see the result of an error at some stage because the canceller is separated from its accidental by an unusual number of notes. For No. 50 we have a concordance which introduces an earlier cancelling symbol. The *Et resurrexit* of No. 83 (Leonel) separates the two symbols by 33 notes and ligatures.

In most cases the notes between an accidental and its canceller may be solmized in the one hexachord suggested by the accidental — occasionally the upper or lower semitones, with or without chromatic alteration, are required. This is probably because the vocal range of most parts is usually fairly limited within a short passage, and because of the availability of one hexachord from another even within the ficta mutations, which could easily account for any notes outside the range of the single hexachord:

Ex. 21

Note here how each implied hexachord descends to a longer note on its ut (compare the Mi-rule, 82). I have discussed the physical position of manuscript accidentals in some detail, showing how various interpretations of other notes may be called for and how the solmization function may realise unusual meanings. Now we have to consider the musical position and effect of the accidental. From what has been said, it will be apparent that I believe the melodic meaning to have been paramount, at least for the performer.

Melodic Context

61. Melodically, manuscript accidentals occur just where one would expect to find them: sharps at upward leading notes, flats at upper returning notes, and the like. But these conventional and obvious points are just those which would be singled out for extempore alteration by melodic rule of thumb: if such a rule existed, as I have hypothesised, why write in the accidental?

I have established (3) that the performers' memory must have played a very important part and that manuscript accidentals must have had some function other than the obvious one, and the application of preplaced accidentals especially implies this. So perhaps does the entering of an accidental in one voice only, causing a vertical difficulty to be remedied by another alteration not written in: the sharpening of the third but not the sixth before fifth and octave in the $\substack{6\text{-}8 \\ 3\text{-}5}$ progression is the obvious situation. Such passages may suggest that a melodic function of accidentals overweighed their vertical one because accidentals which cause rather than resolve vertical problems as the theorists instruct are more likely to have been placed for melodic reasons. For preplaced accidentals we have established some other functions — for example, that of causing a transposition of the system to imply or reject certain other accidentals which could otherwise have been made. Exactly the same function may lie within accidentals other than those preplaced, except that of course the restrictions or alterations implicit can occur only after the note.

62. On occasions, manuscript accidentals may appear in positions where alteration might be expected, but where there might also be ambiguity, for example, when the note occurs elsewhere in the vicinity as an important and uninflected pitch. Looking ahead in the following passage and noting the obviously stronger cadence on F may cause uncertainty about the 'pseudo-cadence' on G:

Ex. 22

No. 36 (fos. 30v - 31): I, 120 Cooke ibid.

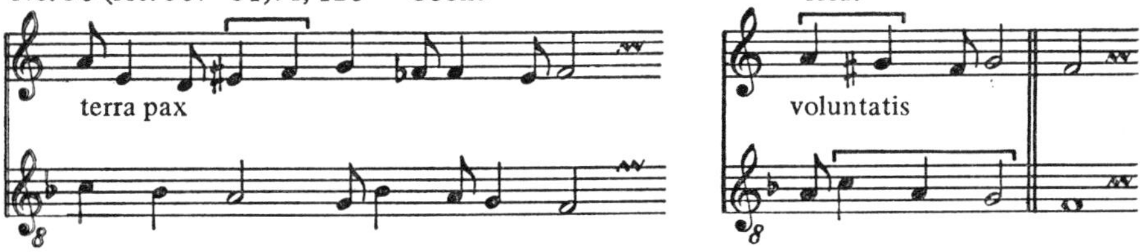

On the other hand, no such reason can be offered for the sharpening of leading notes to final cadences: there can be no question of implying later alterations. The sole ambiguity lies in the choice between a sharpened or a Phrygian cadence, and the latter is restricted to the one available with a recta flat. Cadences to A are Phrygian unless a manuscript accidental is added, because the B of the lowest voice may be flattened within the recta scheme: manuscript G♯s as leading notes in the top voice therefore need no explanation. But final accidentals such as the following are difficult to account for:

Ex. 23

No. 16 (fos. 12v - 13): I, 24 Roy Henry

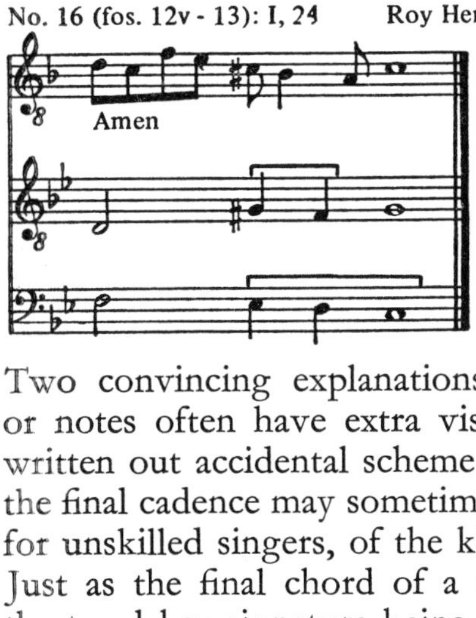

Two convincing explanations have been offered. Final cadences or notes often have extra visual ornamentation, of which a fully written out accidental scheme may be one symptom. Alternatively, the final cadence may sometimes have served as an example, perhaps for unskilled singers, of the kind of accidentals required elsewhere. Just as the final chord of a tonal piece specifies the precise key, the tonal key-signature being ambiguous, so the final cadence may indicate which notes are normally to be preceded by accidentals (see section 92 on Melodic Tonics). A third reason is improbable. In the previous example neither accidental is needed, given a melodic rule for returning notes or leading notes. Indeed, earlier in the piece are many almost identical cadences without the manuscript accidentals. I have earlier made a case for scribal accuracy and also for meaningful rather than haphazard use of such indications. May we take it that in such pieces the normal rules are not to apply unless specially indicated? In other words, leading notes should not be sharpened by extempore practice unless so marked. Where the cadence serves as a model for the whole piece, final accidentals may be distinct from and earlier in time than the others.

63. The melodic contexts in which accidentals occur are shown here with an approximate percentage to indicate their relative order of frequency:

Ex. 24

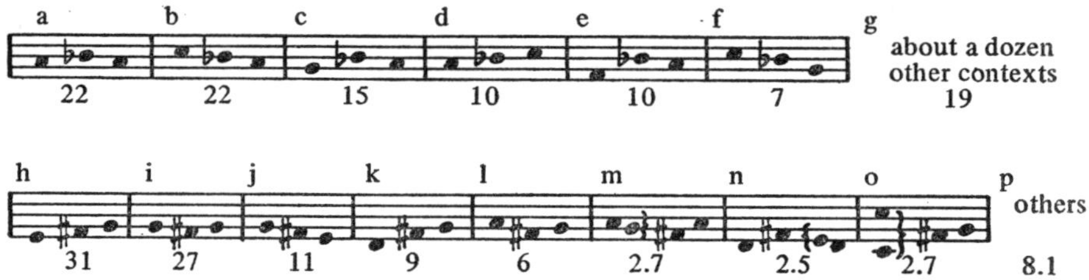

The statistical figures from which these facts were drawn serve mainly to confirm what we can deduce instinctively, and can be only a very approximate guide. Excluded from consideration were restatements of key-signatures after temporary cancellation and accidentals which cancel previous accidentals: the remainder, the majority, are those which disturb rather than restore the normal situation. Since it is difficult to decide whether certain signs are signatures or not, figures for the flats and naturals could vary according to different interpretations: the variation would be moderate. Also omitted were certain very odd or unusual accidentals. A few individual pieces may be responsible for overweighting some areas but there is a sufficiently large number of examples to absorb these bulges, and we are searching only for the general picture, not for the detail.

A distinction by voice, style and key-signature may be made, and the following Table is a very rough guide to the frequency of accidentals in the various combinations in Old Hall:

TABLE V

Numbers in parentheses show the number of preplaced accidentals included in the first figure.

Style and signature	Sign	Top voice	Middle	Lowest
English descant	B♭	1 (1)	8 (2)	41 (15)
	E♭			1
	F♯	50 (15)	6 (3)	1
–,–,–	C♯	12 (7)	4 (1)	1
	G♯	4		
	B♭	7 (4)	1 (1)	
	B♮			1
–,–,♭	F♯	6 (4)	1	
	C♯	1 (1)		
	G♯	1		
Homophonic later descant	B♭	1 (1)		13 (9)
	F♯	19 (12)	1 (1)	
	C♯	4 (3)	6 (1)	1 (1)
–,–,–	G♯		2	
	B♭	2 (1)	1	
	E♭			1
–,–,♭	B♮			1
	F♯	9 (3)		
	C♯	2 (2)	3 (3)	
	B♭	8 (2)	8 (5)	22 (12)
Complex	E♭			3 (1)
	F♯	41 (16)	15 (7)	
–,–,–	C♯	38 (13)	11 (6)	5 (1)
	G♯	14	4 (1)	
	B♭	17 (6)	10 (2)	
	B♮			8 (5)
–,–,♭	F♯	26 (12)	1 (1)	
	C♯	5 (1)	1 (1)	
	B♭	41 (23)		
	E♭		1	2 (1)
	B♮		8 (6)	10 (3)
–,♭,♭,	F♯	37 (16)	5 (1)	1
	C♯	5 (2)	5 (2)	1
	G♯	4 (2)		
	D♯		1 (1)	
	E♭	11 (7)		
	B♮	14 (13)	5 (2)	1
♭, ♭e♭, ♭e♭	E♮		13 (9)	3
	F♯	7 (6)	4 (1)	
	C♯	3		

In strict descant style the recta accidentals fall heavily into the lowest voice, occurring more than twice as often as in the other two voices put together. Top and middle voices have about the same number each, but in the former they occur mainly when the lowest voice has a B♭ signature. We may already see a distinction between the three parts. This is confirmed by the ficta accidentals. There are rather few pieces with key-signatures in the lowest part; cancellations are thus rare and restricted to that voice. Other than these there are almost no ficta accidentals in the voice — a single F♯ and C♯ were noted.

Sharps predominate in the top voice and are more frequent than all recta accidentals combined: F♯s occur three times as often as C♯ and G♯ combined. This proportion is different in the middle voice, whose total number of ficta accidentals is much less: the number of F♯s is less than twice the number of C♯s: no G♯s were recorded.

64. There is definitely a difference in the manuscript chromaticism according to voice: recta flats predominate in the lowest voice, first degree sharps in the top and middle voices, but the latter has a much higher proportion of second degree sharps. The same situation is even more prominent in the homophonic pieces mainly by later composers, rhythmically freer than strict descant. In the top voice there are four times as many F♯s as C♯s and no G♯s: in the middle there are very few F♯s, many C♯s and a few G♯s, but in total they form about a third of the number of sharps altogether in the top voice.

As for sharps, the top voices and contratenor of the complex styles have an exactly similar relationship: the upper voices have many more sharps, rapidly declining in number the further the degree. The contratenor has many fewer altogether but F♯ and C♯ are more nearly equal. Since these styles often have conflicting signatures, naturals occur quite often and are fairly evenly distributed; contratenor and tenor appear to have a larger number only because they often have the signature with the greater number of flats. For the same reason the top voice has a much greater proportion of recta accidentals than the lower voices. In fact, the presence or absence as well as the kind of signature makes a considerable difference in complex styles, and some difference in the other styles. Expected is the drop in sharps as accidentals and the corresponding rise in their equivalent, naturals. Not so easy to understand is the greatly increased proportion of preplaced accidentals in more highly signatured pieces although in (44) I have offered a possible explanation.

Some clues for the editor may emerge. Principally the distribution of accidentals helps to confirm that each voice in all styles should be regarded differently.

The Contratenor[19]

65. In the complex styles tenor and contratenor are usually in the same clef with the same range and signature (but see 32-33 & App. II). Evidently they need to be treated differently because the latter generally cadences upwards, like the upper voices, and thus needs sharps more often. Moreover its melodic character is often very different from that of the tenor. In fact, when it is a typically French contratenor it is hardly a melodic voice at all, using unwieldy leaps and unusual intervals merely for the function of filling out the harmony and rhythm. Are we justified in applying to this voice the same dependence on the hexachord with its purely melodic implications? Probably not. Harmonic function is surely of much more concern. This may give us the clue to certain passages in which the contratenor confuses the issue:

Ex. 25

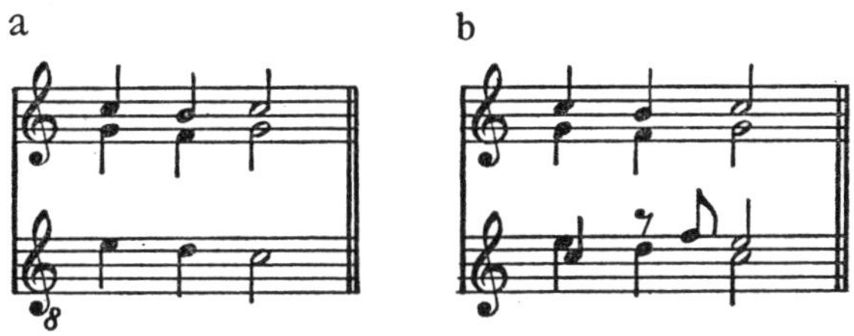

In Ex. 25a the F should clearly be sharp. In 25b the downward leading note of the added contratenor requires an F♮, if considered melodically. Perhaps it should be sharp to conform with the other voices: the resulting leap of an augmented fourth from the preceding C would be questionable only by melodic aesthetics. In a few cases, a false relation may be the correct solution, especially if the contratenor is melodically composed and if there are similar inescapable chromatic clashes elsewhere in the piece. Such clashes probably happened accidentally through erroneous singing and one should remember the undoubted English penchant for them in the sixteenth century.

66. Where he implies that an accidental shows the place for mutation, Prosdocimus pointedly refers only to tenor and discant (41). A French style of contratenor not melodically conceived,

19. See Hughes, "Some Notes..."

and not dependent on the hexachord system, could have no use for preplaced accidentals whose function was to show points of mutation or transposition. If they are present it may be for one of the other reasons mentioned, or else the function of the voice itself has to be questioned.

Here are some examples in which the contratenor has written-in accidentals for purely harmonic reasons, and which are undesirable, or at least unnecessary, in the melodic sense:

Ex. 26

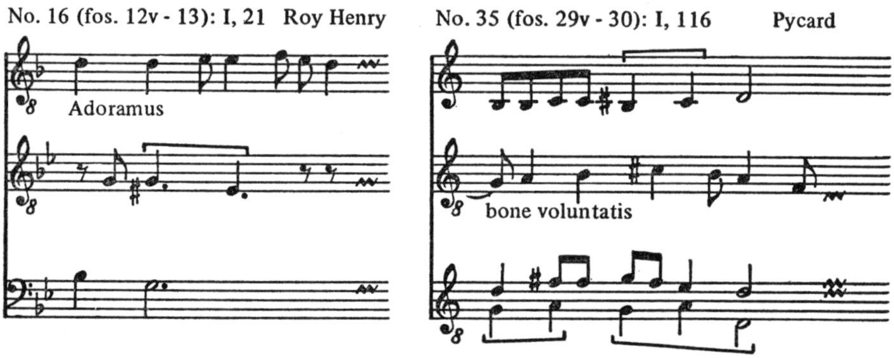

In the contratenor accidentals tend to be added to a quite varied set of melodic situations, in the total range of which they are more or less evenly distributed. Unusual melodic settings are relatively frequent.

The other voices have more accidentals in fewer melodic contexts, and they tend to be concentrated in motives such as ABA, EFG, while others are represented by only the isolated accidental. Unusual melodic contexts occur mostly in pieces like Nos. 36 (Cooke) and 35 (Pycard).

Since melody seems to be of less importance to its purpose, the contratenor should be examined last when the problem of adding or analysing accidentals arises: more important in any investigation of this music are of course the fundamental voices.

Fundamental voices

67. In simple chanson style there is no question: tenor and the upper voice or voices have to be taken first, and their movement has to be corrected. The theorists' neglect of more than two parts when discussing musica ficta may well be because the third part, the contratenor, was regarded as inessential and had to be treated differently. Once tenor and upper voices agree with what the theorists describe, the contratenor may be adjusted, firstly in relation to harmony, making it consonant with the tenor and upper voices as far as chromatic alteration will allow and regardless of melodic movement. It may then be looked at melodically in relation to the tenor and altered to agree with what the theorists state about thirds before fifths, etc., provided that the harmonic consonance is not thereby destroyed.

In descant style there is little problem either: here the tenor and counter have to be taken first, followed by the top voice in relation to the other two. Melodic as well as harmonic aspects need to be examined for the third voice and, given the simplicity of the style, an alteration for one reason is likely to be correct for the other.

68. Isorhythmic pieces are somewhat different: the contratenor is usually not the inessential part of chanson style. Sometimes it cannot be omitted. Its melodic outline is then important: moreover, because of its essential nature accidentals may have to be added before dealing with the upper parts, which thus become dependent on the harmonic foundation of the lower voices. Adjustment of the lower parts according to melodic logic would require all statements of the isorhythmic *color* to have the same chromatic alterations. The presence of manuscript accidentals in the upper voices usually makes this impossible. Similarly, it seems logical to alter canonic voices identically. This, too, is often not possible because of manuscript accidentals or changed harmonic context in the other parts. Contrary to the suggestion for isorhythmic pieces, it may be preferable to examine the canonic voices first, making the lower parts conform to them wherever the latter are not committed by written-in accidentals.

But to preserve, before all else, chromatic identity in successive voices of a canon or in *color* repeats imbues the accidental with an unjustifiable importance. The total result should be of more concern. Like the extemporised ornament of later periods, which can differ in repetitions without destroying the quality of an imitation, the accidental does not change the essence of the melodic line (44). This appears to deny the primacy of the melody. Nevertheless, for the performer horizontal rules must still take precedence at first, but they become of secondary importance relative to the whole texture. The modern editor must emulate performer in the first stage, precentor or listener in the second.

69. Horizontal rules prescribing only diatonic progressions and perfect intervals are certainly too narrow, especially for many contratenor parts, although they may provide the basis for more flexible principles. Manuscript practice itself confirms the use of other intervals. In Old Hall, most common is the chromatic progression, occurring in more than a dozen passages. Although in a few the first pitch also needs alteration, a sufficient number, all in strict descant style, remain unquestionable, showing that such movement was acceptable, if not very common:

Ex. 27

No. 122 (fos. 99v - 100): I, 369 Tyes

Whether or not they should be used in complex styles is difficult to answer, but there are several theorists who give such progressions as a normal part of their discussions.

The tritone caused by manuscript alteration of the second note of an ascending interval is also fairly common if the movement continues upward. Equally divided between top voice and contratenor, about a dozen occur in both descant and complex styles. A few could have the first note altered to perfect the fourth, others could not:

Ex. 28

No. 129 (f. 102v): I, 383 Anon

No. 71 (fos. 59v - 60): I, 195 - 196 Anon

70. The accidental is added in every case so that the vertical third or sixth is sharpened before fifth or octave: none of these is objectionable (though there are two or three others not counted here which are most unusual). Moreover, to correct them would require a ficta accidental whereas manuscript correction of tritones, when effected, is done only by recta means. Here is the only exception noted and the correction by direct manuscript accidental is carefully avoided. The passage sets the words *Maria virgine.*

Ex. 29

No. 62 (f. 50v): I, 185 Typp

No. 81 (Leonel) has two examples of a descending tritone caused by manuscript accidental: both are extremely odd for other reasons. This piece and No. 84 (also by Leonel) have one diminished fifth each, in the contratenor:

Ex. 30

No. 81 (fos. 68v - 69): I, 250 Leonel

No. 84 (fos. 71v - 72): I, 266 Leonel

71. Almost no evidence of the period supports the conventional modern claim that melodic tritones were prohibited in early music: if anything, there are more hints suggesting the opposite conclusion in certain circumstances. The usual theoretical reference is to the vertical interval, associated with the rule forbidding mi against fa on consonances. If there does exist, in the Middle Ages, a clear prohibition of the horizontal form, the rule is not emphasised nor does it appear in sections devoted to ficta, for which such an imperfect interval might be thought to constitute a *causa necessitatis.* Only the impossibility of solmizing the tritone in a normal way suggests that the interval was corrected in most cases. Ser Lorenzo, a practical composer, offers the most obvious enjoinder to avoid the interval in what appears to be a melodic context[20], and an

20. See *L'Antefana di Ser Lorenzo* in "The Music of Fourteenth Century Italy", ed. N. Pirrotta, *Corpus Mensurabilis Musicae* 8, vol. 3, American Institute of Musicology, Rome 1954, p.1, fn.3, and p.xv (facs.). See also Lowinsky's transcriptions and discussion of the piece in Foreword..., pp.v-xxi.

anonymous fifteenth century theorist rejects it when it returns within itself[21]. The same theorist, however, in an obscure and probably defective paragraph seems to suggest it was acceptable when continued in the same direction. More positive evidence of its use is in the musical sources, including examples in treatises. Prosdocimus' example in the *Tractatus de Contrapuncto* (Coussemaker III, 199) is the best known, in which the ligature joining the notes of the interval precludes the assertion that they belong to separate 'examples'[22]. Sources of polyphony, and indeed occasionally plainsong, transmit numerous instances of tritones caused by written-in accidentals, and these normally occur when the line continues in the same direction, or at cadence points, where the inflected pitch serves as a leading note. It is my belief that there is more evidence from all areas to suggest that the interval was melodically acceptable in certain contexts, and that within them the evidence of the music and of manuscript accidentals unmistakably confirms its not infrequent use, and that the necessities of extempore chromatic alteration demand it. To put it in the least radical way: if anything has to be flexible it should be melodic intervals such as the tritone and chromatic progression. The tritone with notes intervening is probably subject to the same adjustment as the direct interval: if continued in the same direction it is acceptable, if continued with a return within itself it should more often be adjusted.

72. For other melodic intervals there is less evidence, and very little indeed in Old Hall itself. Unquestionable diminished fourths by accidental do occur in certain manuscripts (including one English source of slightly later, the Shrewsbury School MS VI) but in Old Hall they are always separated by at least one note, as in the next example. Augmented fifths occur three times in Old Hall, two caused by accidentals whose exact meaning is uncertain. The third is shown here and although confirmed by concordance is, at best, doubtful:

21. See Bent, diss., 415, and Coussemaker IV, 380-381.
22. Lowinsky, "Conflicting Views...", p.202.

Ex. 31

For augmented seconds there is also very uncertain manuscript evidence, and the interval occurs only below the second or third degree sharp in a cadential context:

Ex. 32

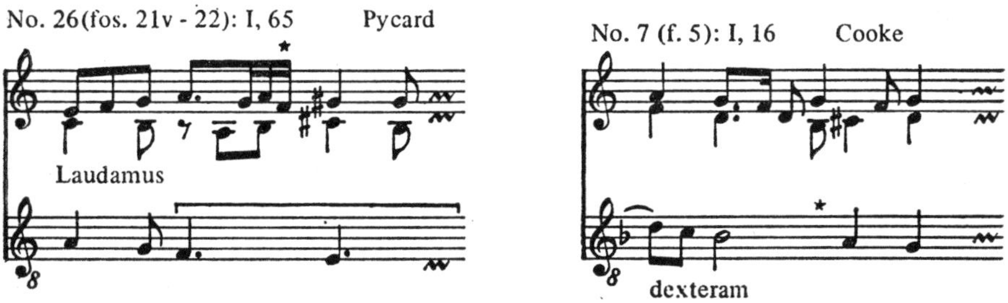

In both of these examples the mi-rule explained in section 82 would help.

Finally I quote a passage in which either an augmented second or a tritone appears inescapable, and the latter should be preferred even though it involves another F♯ elsewhere (also perhaps deriving from the mi-rule):

Ex. 33

No other unusual melodic contexts appear in scribe A's work, but there is at the beginning of *Stella celi*, No. 55, a written manuscript progression D♯ E F. This piece must be considered unusual because of its lavish written-in chromaticism. Its presence in the later layers of the source suggests that it may be a 'demonstration' piece for singers of a decade in which earlier principles had been forgotten.

Purposes for Manuscript Accidentals

73. Chromatic alteration was probably carried out by melodic principles for harmonic ends. The two elements are often inseparable, in which case the idea of movement from one 'chord' to another even more perfect 'chord' is often the reason for the accidental. To study the harmonic context we have to decide what is acceptable as a vertical interval. To contemporary theorists the sole interval unacceptable is the 'unperfect' perfect consonance, solmized with mi and fa simultaneously. We assume that all augmented or diminished perfect intervals are equally unacceptable, whether solmized mi against fa or with other syllables. This assumption has no foundation but appears justified. Generally, then, diminished and augmented harmonies are undesirable. In the two chord progressions just referred to, the concept of degrees of perfection is introduced, rendering the first chord better when it is as close as possible to the perfect consonance. However, the only vertical combination definitely unavailable for the first chord is the augmented sixth, whose simultaneous solmization of mi against fa would entail the forbidden mi against fa on the following consonance:
G♯-mi A-fa
B♭-fa A-mi. Margaret Bent has elucidated this point in more detail (diss., 418-419). Only two vertical combinations, then, are seen as unacceptable: the augmented sixth, and the diminished or augmented perfect consonance. But as a matter of practical necessity, since it is impossible to 'correct' all such instances, the latter must be accepted if brief or caused by ornamental anticipations or passing-notes, especially when between voices other than the two fundamental parts.

74. An analysis of manuscript chromaticism taking into account both melodic and harmonic contexts reveals the following categories:

1) accidentals needed to correct a harmonic or melodic interval, and which create neither a melodic problem for the singer nor a harmonic one for precentor or modern editor,

2) accidentals which have a direct musical effect but which are not needed for any theoretical or practical reason,

3) accidentals which may or may not be needed for theoretical or practical reasons but which in any case are difficult or impossible to interpret and whose context is difficult to emend satisfactorily,

4) accidentals which have no direct effect and which are meaningless according to modern interpretation.

Each of these categories may occur in its simplest form or may be made more complicated by ornaments such as suspensions, anticipations or syncopated anticipations, of the chromatically altered note or of the cadence note itself. Each of these ornaments usually involves an imperfect vertical consonance which, as an ornament, may be ignored[23]. Consecutive false relations are so frequent as to be a perfectly normal part of the technique. The next example shows the first kind of accidental with some of the possible ornaments, the asterisks marking augmented or diminished consonances:

Ex. 34

In some circumstances it may be possible and desirable to remedy the imperfection of example 34c by the mi-rule (82), but only when other difficulties make the passage unacceptable as it stands.

75. Category 1 may be divided into three kinds. In the first, the manuscript accidental is entirely correct (within the limits established) by itself and the context needs no further adjustment. No further discussion need be given and it is entirely the most common situation, accounting for almost half the total of all manuscript accidentals. With certain other examples the context has to be altered, and may be done so easily by either melodic or harmonic rules: the overwhelmingly common example of this is the $^{6\text{-}8}_{3\text{-}5}$ cadence with only the sixth sharpened, causing an augmented fourth vertically. Sometimes the third only is sharpened, giving a diminished fourth, or the upper parts are inverted, $^{10\text{-}12}_{6\text{-}8}$, giving

23. Although it dates from a period earlier than ours, a statement such as Garlandia's may relate to the same kind of musical situation: *a discord is never placed before a perfect consonance except because of a musical ornament* (...nunquam ponitur discordantia ante perfectam concordantiam nisi causa coloris musice.) Coussemaker I, 106.

diminished or augmented fifth. All of these situations are easy to remedy, although a few will involve tritone or chromatic movement in the voice which is uninflected in the manuscript: the 'omission' of some necessary accidentals may have been in order to avoid giving unusual progressions the sanction of written authority. A few others will involve 'awkward' melodic movement in a non-essential contratenor. None of these reasons in itself is sufficient to call for the introduction of an imperfect vertical interval or a false relation, although sometimes the decision is somewhat difficult if the melodic line begins to look very odd, and especially if the optional or later-added nature of some contratenors is considered:

Ex. 35

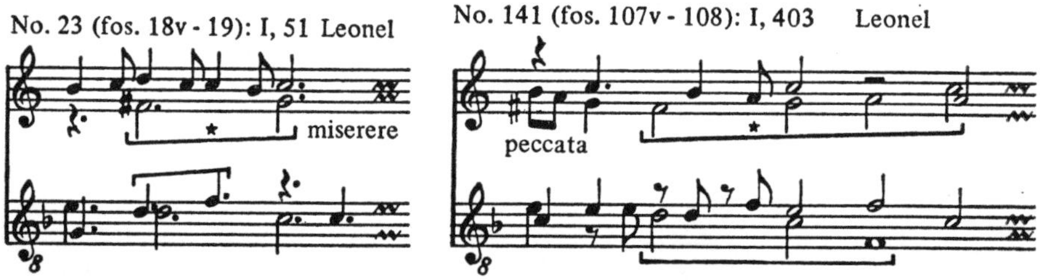

I see no objection to sharpening the contratenor F in the first passage, and while the second is a little more questionable because of the following F♮, in the absence of other false relations in the piece, the contratenor F here might also be sharpened. In the following example we may have the superimposition of two layers of accidentals: the B♮ calls for F♯ above, while the preplaced B♭ suggests F♮-ut:

Ex. 36

Occasionally whether to correct or not may seem entirely dependent on choice — in which case *causa pulchritudinis* may be invoked.

76. The third kind of accidental within category 1 is that in which the accidental is necessary but creates an imperfect vertical interval either as a rather solid passing-note, or even as an essential note. The three basic figures are these:

Ex. 37

It is perfectly possible to avoid the imperfect harmony by sharpening the C, although such a procedure would often cause an obtrusively awkward melodic line, especially in the upper voice: such a line, although permissible in a non-essential contratenor and perhaps in a truly inner part, is not aurally agreeable in a fundamental voice. Such a judgment is, of course, entirely personal and may reflect values totally opposed to those of medieval musicians. But there are a fair number of imperfect intervals of this nature, the alteration of which would be quite impossible: of the same kind, in cadences to A, the B♭ and E♮ interval is not uncommon especially in descant style. Similarly, the passing or essential imperfect interval expanding to a sixth or closing to a third seems within the normal vocabulary. Correction of such brief or idiomatic imperfections often results in other equally 'bad' intervals:

Ex. 38

No. 110 (f. 89): I, 345 Typp

Others cannot be remedied without producing false relations:

Ex. 39

No. 128 (f. 102): I, 381 Anon.

No. 118 (fos. 96v - 97): I, 357 Leonel

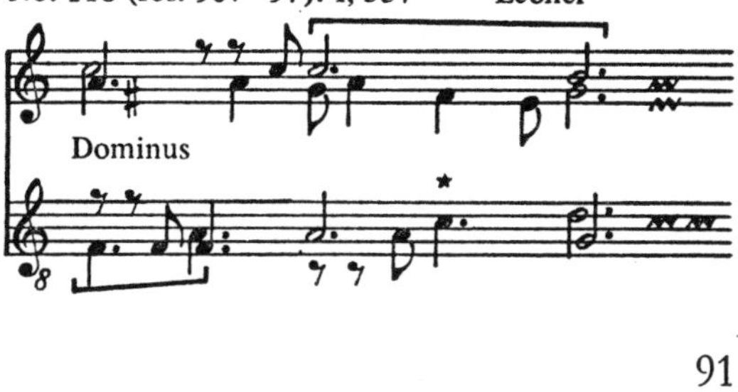

Ex. 39 cont.

No. 61 (f. 48v): I, 181 Chirbury

(♮ in lower voice only)

Many of those similar to the first passage here may be subject to the half-sharpening rule (78) but unless other factors intrude, it is probably better to accept the imperfect interval. Often, as in the second passage, another voice is affected and the normal sharpening of the third before fifth cannot take place except where false relations are inescapable and are indicated elsewhere in the piece.

77. Category 2 may also be divided into the same three kinds: those which can stand entirely by themselves; those which call for a normal chromatic alteration of the context; and the very rare few with which an imperfect interval is acceptable. We do not need to examine each of these kinds since the category may be treated in an overall manner. These accidentals are not required for the perfection of any interval, melodic or vertical. Some occur in predictable positions — e.g., flats in a descending melodic line, sharps in the final chord of a section. Flats of this kind are quite often followed by a resting point on A or F, sharps by one on G or D:

Ex. 40

No. 81 (fos. 68v - 69): I, 250 Leonel

No. 56 (fos. 41 - 42): I, 148 Anon.

This category is particularly interesting since, not being required for obligatory alteration, the accidental may be present for purely aesthetic reasons: it may be *causa pulchritudinis*. I have already mentioned one which may have been added for a similar reason, the aesthetic of heightened text illustration, in No. 123 (section 36). Occasionally a sharp may be placed to give a major third prominently in the upper voice, perhaps a consciously sought effect of the English composers. An aesthetic function may be even more likely when the manuscript accidental deliberately goes against the theoretical rules, as in the third of the following passages where it is perhaps deliberately to imply a chromatic alteration which would otherwise not be made:

Ex. 41

No. 84 (fos. 71v - 72): I, 264 Leonel

No. 77 (fos. 64v - 65): I, 221 Anon

No. 61 (fos. 48v - 50): I, 179 - 180 Chirbury

No. 106 (f. 87): I, 337 Typp

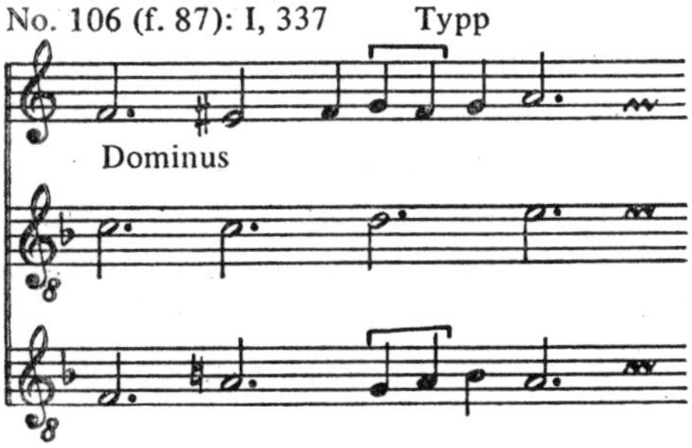

78. Category 3 is a small but important group, being accidentals which are definitely not good as they stand, and whose context cannot be altered easily. They are concentrated in a number of pieces such as Nos. 28 & 35, Pycard; and 81, Leonel. We cannot examine all of them, and a few examples must suffice to illustrate some unusual although logical procedures for dealing with intransigent situations.

a) *Half-sharpening.* By analogy with chromatic sharpening of a repeated pitch, it may be necessary to sharpen a held note at its mid-point, or at some other suitable place. This is the only rational way of resolving such passages as the first given below—if all the parts are to be performed together, not necessarily a correct assumption[24] — and it is the simplest way in the second passage. Until confirmation is available, such a method should be regarded as a last resort.

Ex. 42

No. 28 (fos. 22v - 23): I, 81 - 82 Pycard

No. 26 (fos. 21v - 22): I, 69 Pycard

Note that both of these passages are by Pycard. In the first the actual place for half-sharpening is a matter of choice: the prominent declamation of *virginis* might be a matter to consider.

79. b) *Simultaneous false relations.* Consecutive false relations are quite acceptable. Simultaneously, they seem unavoidable in certain passages but should probably be used only if the piece has many accidentals, and a number of similar difficult passages occur. In short, the chromatic style must be consistent within the piece. No. 36 (Cooke) comes to mind immediately; another tricky example is drawn from No. 77 (anon.):

Ex. 43

No. 36 (fos. 30v - 31): I, 121 Cooke

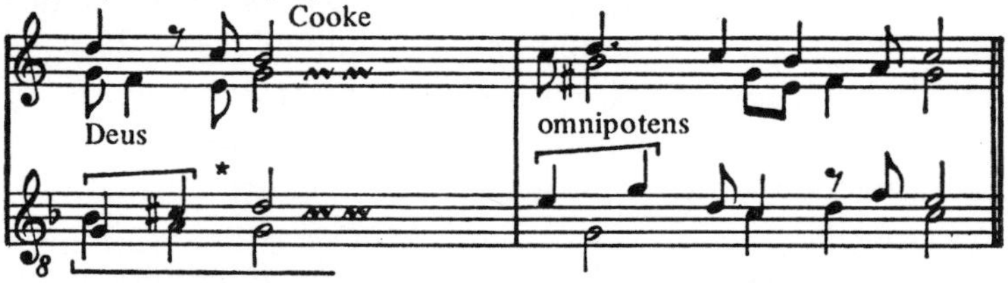

24. Hughes, "Some Notes...", *passim*. See also *Journal of the American Musicological Society* VIII, 1955, p.38.

Ex. 43 cont.

ibid.; I, 123

A noticeable element in No. 36 is that the potential false relations are not caused each time by an accidental in the same part: in one place the chromatically altered note is in the contratenor, in another the second upper part, and so on. This suggests an inherent and integral interest in a special effect. If the difficult notes had appeared only in one part, the problem could result from melodic alteration of that part, without the corresponding and necessary harmonic adjustment. The only false relation in which both notes have manuscript accidentals occurs in this piece, shown in the third passage quoted. The most difficult and frequent cross-relations occur in No. 75 (anon.), a canon:

80. c) *Canonic pieces.* It is not clear whether manuscript accidentals in canonic parts are to apply to all of the voices forming the canon, or to only the leader or one of the consequents. In practice it seems that more often the accidental works for the leader but not always for the others. May this be a hint that these pieces could be performed without the canonic followers? Nos. 35 (Pycard) and 75 (anon.) are the two most complex, and in these it is most frequently the contratenor which causes problems of vertical adjustment; if its melodic line is ignored sometimes the passage is easier to correct. The emendation of other clashes may be facilitated at times by omitting one from, or adding an accidental to, some but not all of the canonic parts. Canonic strictness is thus broken. It may be argued that the melodic motivation is so strong that every attempt should be made to preserve canonic identity but the practicalities of the matter frequently require the most extreme distortions of the normal vocabulary in order to achieve this ideal. In any case, one may legitimately enquire whether the mathematics and enigmatics of canonic writing were in the composer's mind more than the aesthetics and the practical result. Mathematics is even more the motivation in No. 75, a mensural canon. It can even be postulated that this piece is simply an exercise of ingenuity in making the canonic parts mensurally different and yet each correct with the same tenor, with which each part by itself forms good (or with chromatic alterations potentially good) counterpoint. Each frequently clashes with the contratenor, whose melodic line must be considerably changed in order to achieve harmonic perfection. It is an odd fact that if all the C♯s are omitted from the canonic parts hardly any extra alterations need to be made. One passage is beyond solution if the contratenor and all the other parts were sung:

Ex. 44

81. d) *Solmization accidentals*. On a few rare occasions an accidental makes no sense by any normal standards, but an acceptable result can be obtained if it is taken to mean a re-arrangement of the context to form the right hexachord about its uninflected pitch. That is, a sharp will not mean 'raise the note a semitone' but 'the note above has to be fa and must be lowered to make it a semitone away'. As stated this procedure is perfectly in accordance with theoretical statements (20). The procedure works particularly well in two pieces, both by Pycard:

Ex. 45

In both passages (and an earlier very similar one in No. 76) the C♯ will not work sensibly, but taking it to mean "C is mi in the hexachord on A♭" gives D♭ B♭ and A♭, which are more tolerable although it is necessary to alter the other parts by aural analogy. Since No. 76 has a whole section in which an abstruse technical transposition into a very distant flat key-signature has been postulated[25], the Phrygian cadence to C does not appear out of the chromatic style.

The following passage by Leonel is suspicious but perhaps best treated as though the sharp were a normal accidental, despite the following C♮ chord:

Ex. 46

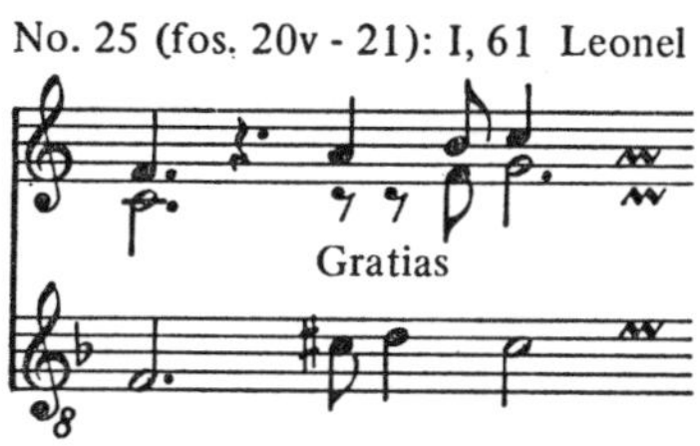

82. A few others could perhaps be interpretated as solmization accidentals, but none as satisfactorily as the first two quoted. It is probably significant that the two or three which do work (as well as those questioned and discarded) are all sharps: the three quoted are C♯s. Sharps give flats as the result of this kind of hexachord shifting and, more important, they give ficta flats. We have seen that such accidentals are not used (55-56): was this method a trick to circumvent the prohibition?

e) *Mi-rule*. A further last resort useful in a number of awkward

25. See notes to this piece in the new edition of Old Hall, vol. III.

contexts I have called the mi-rule. This simply means that, given a descending line in the lowest part, it may be useful to regard as ut a noticeably strong resting point, the third above which, where it is not already major, being sharpened to give mi. The most frequent context in which this would resolve difficulty can easily be quoted:

Ex. 47

Sharpening the lower F would allow the F and G of the top voice, and the C of the middle voice to be sharpened, avoiding the augmented melodic second and augmented fifth otherwise needed to approach the perfect intervals. Three passages will serve to show the application of this:

Ex. 48

No. 62 (f. 50): I, 184
Typp

No. 77 (fos. 64v - 65): I, 218 Anon.

No. 26 (fos. 21v - 22): I, 65 Pycard

83. Category 4, accidentals which have neither effect nor meaning according to modern interpretation, is a small group of perhaps a dozen. It should be clear from the preceding pages that a single symbol can have one or more of several meanings. An apparently unnecessary re-statement of a key-signature may imply 'move from the hexachord on ut shown by the flat in the signature to the one on fa shown by this symbol'. An apparently unnecessary

B♮ in a non-signatured part may mean 'do not apply a recta flat to this note'. In the following excellent example a recta E♭ leading to the D might otherwise have been required:

Ex. 49

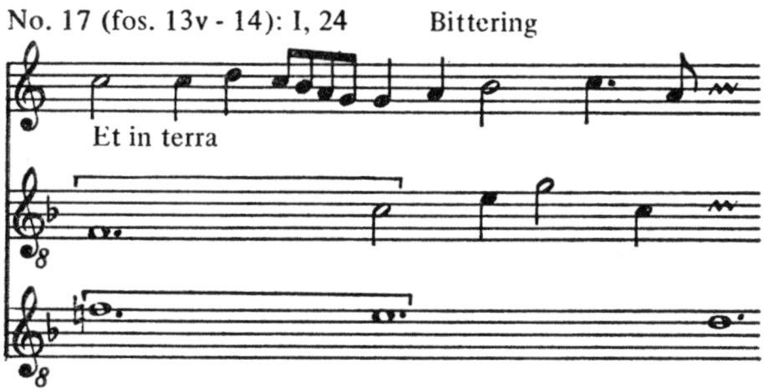

These symbols are limited in Old Hall to B♭, B♮-♯, E♭, E♮-♯, which reinforces the suspicion that hexachords and recta notes are limited and suggested by this method. Here is a slightly different example, in which a Phrygian and recta cadence should be preferred:

Ex. 50

In the next quoted passage is an accidental which probably serves a pitch or solmizing function, keeping the C natural as fa, although it has no following B to refer to:

Ex. 51

No. 75 (fos. 62v - 63): I, 207 Anon.

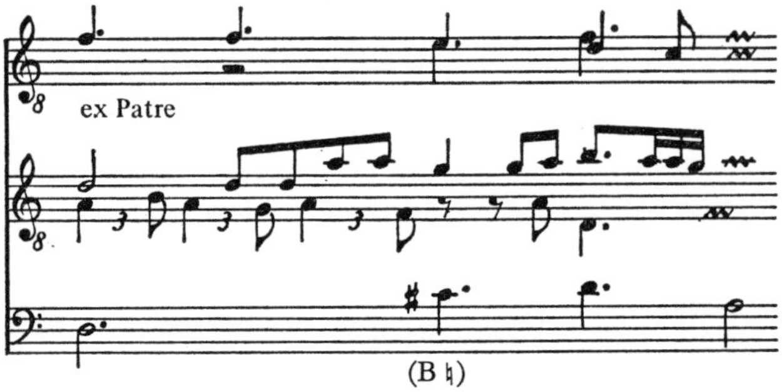

On the other hand, no convincing explanation can be offered for the A♯ above the final F in No. 101 (f.84v, anon.); however, one may compare several pieces in which accidentals stand above the final note or ligature of one section and before the manuscript stroke separating it from the next section (e.g., Appendix I, No. 8, bar 34).

Rhythm and Text

84. No statistics have been kept, but it is quite clear that almost all accidentals affect notes of a *semibrevis* or longer. The inflection therefore usually begins the perfection, triple or duple, reinforcing the proposition that in the rhythmic scheme this is the important point when one examines extempore chromatic addition. Although only the most imprecise of guides, there may even be a hint as to speed, that is, to the value of the *tactus*, or to the rhythmic movement within the perfection; for instance, whether a hemiola should be felt in its own rhythm or within the metre it is disturbing. In Ex. 52 which note should have the feeling of accent?

Ex. 52

No. 122 (fos. 99v - 100): I, 372 Tyes

In this passage with its imperfect interval on a manuscript *semibrevis* the *tactus* should perhaps be on the (perfect) *brevis*. There is nothing in the piece to make this difficult, and in fact nearly all the manuscript accidentals, as in the example, are preplaced so that they stand before a *brevis* perfection rather than within it. The careful indication of mensural grouping, regardless of accidentals, may have a similar bearing on speed.

It is also noticeable that accidentals affecting notes of a *minima* or shorter are usually 'off the perfection' and it is these shorter values which frequently cause rather than resolve imperfections and dissonances:

Ex. 53

No. 25 (fos. 20v - 21): I, 61
Leonel

No. 26 (fos. 21v - 22): I, 66
Pycard

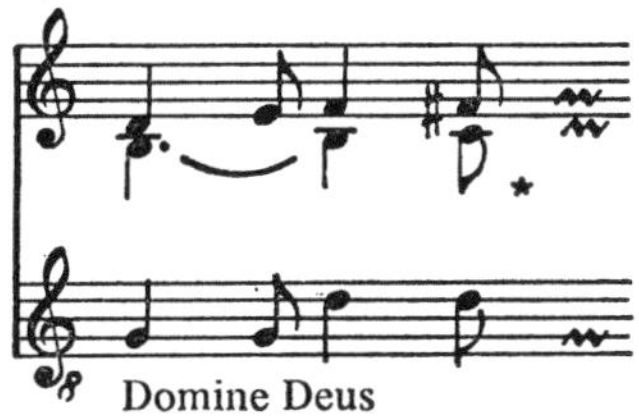

No. 36 (fos. 30v - 31): I, 122 Cooke

No. 84 (fos. 71v - 72): I, 266
Leonel

85. Many of the awkward passages quoted earlier involve an accidental on a *minima*. Certain pieces in Old Hall place many accidentals on this value: amongst the complex styles Nos. 25 (Leonel), 36 (Cooke), 81 & 84 (Leonel) are notable in this respect and have been singled out earlier. Occasionally when proportional augmentation or diminution of a part is present the accidentals may hint at the *integer valor*, which of course is closely related to the *tactus*.

If it is present or important at all, does this association between accidental and rhythm have any relation to text? Impossible to say in our present state of knowledge but the conventional answer would be negative. Nevertheless there is a good deal of evidence that text underlay is careful and accurate in Old Hall (Bent, diss., 111f.). I have suggested that occasionally the text, or rather a specific word, might have been important, and certainly words like *Jesu Christe* or *Maria virgine* are sometimes singled out for long notes and chromatic inflection. Other than these clear examples and some vague hints, no definite evidence can be shown at the present time.

CONCLUSION

86. Only in a very few pieces or those with too few accidentals for the fact to be significant do the accidentals fall into any pattern. In order to produce the preceding pages I have examined and collated such features as the following: symbol, status (recta or ficta), colour, physical position, melodic context, harmonic context, voice, style, text, cadence, rhythm, mensuration, and composer. The use of a key-sort system of analysis allowed many of the permutations to be investigated, but no useful correlations were noted other than those mentioned. Certain hints not strong enough to be remarked here did emerge and may be worth pursuing with an analytical procedure of more precision. The lack of a precedent for such analysis, and ignorance of the questions which needed to be asked, made the forging of an accurate critical tool an almost insurmountable difficulty. A computer could examine more possibilities, more complex relationships. But the nature of an extemporised or even a recorded art is too inconsistent for precise evaluation by a logical instrument. To produce answers this tool of investigation must be fed with the right information, and must be asked the right questions, both matters which call for human judgment. I hope that these pages may be a starting point. Analysis of manuscript chromatic alteration may yet become a valuable and accepted tool of musical scholarship: indeed I believe that it must do so.

Practical suggestions for editors

87. There is perhaps no intrinsic reason why extempore additions should follow the same principles as manuscript accidentals and one could argue that the reason for them is inherently different. But since we have no other guides than those we have discussed, it would be foolish to ignore what can be learnt from what is written into the manuscripts.

88. Analysis of written-in accidentals should evaluate the following:

i) key-signatures and omissions at new lines and sections, and the possibility of latent signatures, and

ii) the recta notes implied by these factors,

iii) the general chromatic style,

iv) note-grouping, rhythmic position of, and average note length affected by, accidentals, in order to establish a speed,

v) visual position of symbols, remembering that in score notation one performer may be able to see the accidentals of another part,

vi) the textual position,

vii) the need for visual reminders, assuming that some rules of melodic thumb existed. If the need appears nil, evaluate

viii) the possibility that some symbols are written in to avoid placing other more unusual or distant accidentals, and

ix) their possible functions as pitch indicators or as patterns for the rest of the piece.

Evaluate also

x) the possibility of solmizing accidentals in close horizontal proximity, and the vertical compatibility of simultaneous accidentals, in order to judge whether different layers are involved. This may invalidate some of the manuscript additions,

xi) the possibility that omission of a complete voice, especially the contratenor, would alleviate difficult passages. This factor, too, might invalidate some manuscript accidentals.

xii) the possibility that unusual key-signatures might indicate transposition of the whole texture (see App. II).

89. The addition of further chromaticism should be governed by these policies:

a) prefer recta accidentals,

b) avoid ficta flats unless legitimized by a relevant recta flat,

c) new lines or sections may specify changes in transposition or signature,

d) accidentals have a once-only effect, but the hexachord or system implied by flats may continue,

e) only essential notes between fundamental voices need considering for vertical perfection — ornaments may be ignored — and this is more important at

f) the beginnings of mensural perfections (perhaps half-perfections) while notes "off the beat" are less significant,

g) the fundamental duet should be considered first and

h) the tenor, or given part, is to some extent regarded as fixed, so that

i) the upper voice adjusts to it rather than the opposite,

j) the inessential contratenor must be considered last and for it vertical necessities take precedence over its melodic line, but not over a) and b) above,

k) brief imperfect intervals are acceptable, especially if they are not at the beginning of a perfection.

90. Each specific piece requires specific modifications of these general rules, depending on its style, chromaticism, lay-out, performance by soloists or choir, and many other factors. Application of general principles prepared in advance as though extemporisation were something fixed beforehand, like notation, is bound to meet with difficulties, if not failure. In the same way, a modern score, with its consistent key-signature, barring and beaming, etc., practically forces the editor into other prejudices. He should work in the first stages from the original source rather than from transcription: medieval notation was sufficiently concise for a whole phrase to be within a single eye-span. Thus, from the original, long melodic contours can be appreciated and assessed as complete musical sentences rather than as a series of individual notes or motives which the spacing of modern transcription presents visually. For an extempore practice to have been feasible, the eye must have been able to perceive instantaneously the important notes upon which rules of melodic thumb could be based.

From the original the editor must begin with the fundamental voices one at a time. Only normal perfect melodic intervals should be used in this stage, but certain imperfect ones may be considered as later harmonic needs make necessary. The second stage should be that of considering the counterpoint of fundamental parts together, making it agree with theoretical requirements about intervals preceding perfect intervals, as well as points e), f) and k) of the above list. Since it is rarely possible to establish at this stage which of two upper parts is the fundamental, it may be necessary first to consider one upper voice and the tenor then the other with tenor, and only then to resolve any conflicts in the three taken together. The last stage should examine the harmonic aspect of the whole texture including the contratenor (or the final part, depending on the style), preferring to alter that voice rather than any other, but avoiding really awkward melodic intervals if an alternative is available within the limitations stated. Correction of passages in which the manuscript is already committed by a written accidental may have to rely on modifications of the above procedure.

91. The following list of practical suggestions for the extrication of insoluble difficulty incorporates some unproven theories; it is surely better to fall back on some principle which may be more justified than completely arbitrary alteration. The five suggestions are these:

l) half-sharpening,

m) simultaneous false relations,

n) change the pitch of the hexachord rather than of the note itself,

o) the mi-rule,

p) implication or restriction of other accidentals by manuscript accidental.

We now have to examine the precise musical position for chromatic alteration of the fundamental voices. Since no significant improvements have been incorporated into the policy proposed for and printed in Vol. I of the new edition of Old Hall most of the following paragraphs are a reprint of that policy, with the permission of Armen Carapetyan, the general editor, American Institute of Musicology, and of the co-author and co-formulator of the policy, Mrs Margaret Bent.

92. On the evidence of accidentals appearing in the manuscript and of the statements of theorists, ficta seems to be concerned with cadences (or cadential figures) and is applied principally to the notes leading to those cadences. The melodic conformation of a cadence can nearly always be recognised without reference to the other parts, though the precise treatment may have to be altered when these are added. Notes having a cadential function will be referred to as melodic tonics. These are normally restricted to the musica recta pitches. Such notes are considered to have a tonic function when they are

a) approached by step (or by a conventional and recognisable ornament in place of the step) from above (lower part) or below (upper parts)

b) on the first note of a breve in C or O, occasionally of a semibreve when these measures are irregular, or of a semibreve in Ͼ or ⊙.

They may also have a tonic function in other melodic situations which are less clearly cadences: in such cases the other voices will normally have obvious cadential figures. However, text or the placing of another nearby and perhaps stronger cadence are other factors which may influence the decision to add ficta. These are melodic matters: there will usually be at least one other part to strengthen and confirm the cadential function. Harmonically a cadence is taken to be,

a) principally, the $^{6\text{-}8}_{3\text{-}5}$ progression, and embellished forms

b) secondarily, the 6-8 or 3-5, or the $^{6\text{-}8}_{3\text{-}5}$ progression plus another less standardised melodic line which may, for example, proceed to the third of the cadence rather than to the fifth. Such secondary cadences will normally have the same relevance as primary cadences, but not necessarily so, depending on the melodic and rhythmic pull of the individual parts.

Either kind of cadence terminates a phrase, which may be defined for present purposes as the area between one cadence and the final chord of the next, or the area from one note after one melodic cadence to the final note of the next.

Cadences, then, consist of at least two elements, both melodically and vertically: the cadence chord and its preceding chord, and in each voice the melodic tonic and its leading note. It is the leading notes which are the most susceptible to the application of unwritten accidentals. Melodically in the upper voices they will be lower returning notes, notes approached from below or above, stepwise or by leap, but always a semitone from their tonic and thus sharp — unless the leading note of the lower voice may be flattened by a recta note. Vertically they are the upper notes of thirds and sixths preceding fifths and octaves — the progression which figures so largely in the ficta examples of Ugolino and Prosdocimus. In the lowest voice flat and downward leading notes will be more prominent than in the upper parts, although sharp leading notes will still occur.

93. Which of the possible notes are melodic tonics in a given piece or section of a piece, and thus which are the leading notes likely to have unwritten accidentals applied, depends on the melodic range of the voice, its key-signature and on the hexachord basis apparently implied by those features and by the presence of incidental manuscript accidentals. Thus a three-part piece with no key-signature, and with melodic ranges implied by the clefs C_1 C_3 C_5 — i.e., each range a fifth lower than its neighbour, as in descant style, would probably imply the following scheme:

top voice	B-C	F♯-G	C♯-D		G-A
middle voice	F♯-G	C♯-D	G♯-A	but	D-A
lowest voice	D-C	A-G	E-D		B♭-A

In this case the availability of B♭ as a recta note would indicate Phrygian rather than sharp cadences to A. The lowest voice would also have sharp upward leading notes available. The manuscript addition of an unexpected sharp, apparently unnecessary because implied in the above scheme, may in fact be to shift the whole scheme sharpwards, introducing the G♯-A, D♯-E melodic cadences in the upper parts, and reducing the lowest voice B♭-A to B♮-A.

In the complex styles of chanson, isorhythm and canon the tenor clearly has to have a scheme different from that of the upper voices: as the lowest sounding part at cadences, it naturally descends rather than ascends to the melodic tonic. It will therefore tend to take a natural or a recta flat role at cadences, although sharps will be available for other points. The middle voice in many cases is in the same range and has the same signature as the lowest part although it clearly has more opportunity to behave like an upper voice: its cadences, for example, will rise rather than fall and thus be subject more to sharpening. And, its range being lower than that of the true upper part, its scheme will include the sharp one degree further away.

A clef and key-signature arrangement of C_3♭ C_5♭♭ C_5♭♭ probably implies the following scheme:

top voice	B♮-C	F-G	E♮-F	D-C	C♯-D	(♯ in MS)
middle voice	F♯-G	C-D	B♮-C	G-A or	G♯-A	(♯ by ficta)
lowest voice	D-C	A♭-G	G-F	E♭-D	E♮-D	(♯ by ficta)

The above examples are too simple: in practice obvious cadences other than those on normal melodic tonics, manuscript accidentals, presence of plainsong, possibly even the mode, may have to be taken into account.

94. A few other points need emphasis. Manuscript accidentals are frequently added to long notes, whether leading notes or not, usually in certain text situations such as *Jesu Christe* or *Maria virgine*. Where suitable, accidentals may be applied to similar passages left without chromaticism. Also, at occasional points, an accidental may be introduced according to neither musica recta nor the leading note principle, nor according to text: it may be, for example, a sharp to avert a melodic tritone where a recta flat is not suitable. Such additions would be rare: some would be in contexts immediately recognisable to the performer, others dependent only on the singer's memory.

It remains to state more clearly and with more limitations how the principles may be applied and what are the reasons, usually vertical, for failure to apply them. This section, for the sake of clarity, is presented as a set of rules (which must be interpreted flexibly). The upper voices include the contratenor even where that voice is in the same clef as the tenor; the lowest voice is the counter in descant style and the tenor in the other styles: certain exceptions may occur.

Rules for Editorial Accidentals

95. The first step must be to decide for each individual piece or section of a piece what are the relevant ficta and recta accidentals available to and suitable for each voice.

I: *Musica recta*

Use recta rather than ficta accidentals unless a solution is available only with the latter, or where the latter produces a better result (e.g., if a single recta accidental entails later ficta alterations which a single ficta accidental does not, the latter may be preferred).

Upper voices

Use a recta accidental in the following contexts:

a) to perfect a strong vertical fifth or octave,

b) in a flattish situation, especially in an upper returning note idiom, provided that no vertical fifths or octaves are thereby imperfected. The reader is warned that the rule about 'una nota super la semper est canendum fa' is not given in this or any similar form by contemporary writers on the subject,

c) where necessary to avert the melodic tritone, direct or with intervening notes, when it returns within itself, provided that no vertical fifths or octaves are thereby imperfected. When the interval continues in the same direction, the need to correct it is much less cogent.

Except

i) where a stronger leading note function exists.

Lowest voice

Use a recta accidental

a) for a note descending onto a melodic tonic. This implies a preference for Phrygian cadences where there is otherwise an equal choice between sharps in the upper voices and a flat in the lowest voice,

Except

i) where necessary or unavoidable ficta in the upper voices would give rise to augmented sixths or thirds with it,

ii) where there have already been sharps (manuscript or editorial) in the same phrase,

iii) where to do so would incur vertical imperfect unison, fifth or octave with the upper voices,

[Use a recta accidental]

b) to perfect a melodic interval which returns within itself or has no leading note function,

c) to perfect vertical unisons, fifths, octaves.

II. *Musica ficta*

96. Apply ficta accidentals elsewhere, under the following conditions:

Upper voices

A] sharpen leading notes

Except

i) in a cadence which is unavoidably Phrygian by recta notes, as in this table:

key signature
of lowest
voice

—	D E A B F E	G A D E B[♭] A		
♭	ditto	ditto	C D G A E[♭] D	
♭♭	ditto	ditto	ditto	F G C D A[♭] G

ii) where to do so would produce a vertical imperfect unison, fifth, octave, etc. In this case a chromatic melodic step may be introduced if the note is repeated, and by extension the midway sharpening of a very long note (especially in the lower voices) may be considered, and sometimes appears unavoidable.

iii) where to do so would incur two adjacent melodic semitone steps in the same direction (e.g., A B♭ A G♯ A) except where unavoidable or written into the manuscript.

B] a) add a sharp to avoid the melodic tritone which returns within itself, where recta is not a reasonable alternative.

b) where sharpening of the leading note would incur an augmented second, sharpen the note below the leading note as well (and its octave in another part if necessary).

C] add a sharp to avoid a vertical imperfect unison or octave, also to perfect fifths (less important), particularly on strong beats or for long duration. Exceptions may occur

i) when the two voices concerned move in contrary motion.

ii) for those resulting from slight anticipations in recognisable ornaments.

Lowest voice

As above, sharpen leading notes. But this voice is likely to be one or more degrees flatwards and therefore to make more use of recta. The same melodic and vertical rules apply.

97. None of the above rules need apply over the join of two phrases as defined above: i.e., the first note of a phrase is not conditioned by the final notes of the previous phrase. On the other hand the final note of a phrase may occasionally be affected by the first note of the next phrase, especially if the cadence contains a third.

A special problem arises with canonic pieces, and with isorhythmic tenors (and occasionally contratenors): both of these techniques involve the exact repetition of a melodic line in different vertical contexts. It is not usually possible to retain the melodic application of accidentals intact for each statement: in other words, here, vertical considerations have to be taken as the more important.

The validity of such detailed rules should be questioned. But they are only a starting point, and provided sufficient flexibility is introduced by some means (in this case by reliance on the medieval memory), a clearly stated set of principles can be the only foundation from which to build a system with some consistency and predictability.

Argument about such detailed application of flexible rules seems pointless: few scholars would suggest that a single unvarying system could or should be introduced. By its very nature as a performing practice, the addition of accidentals must have contained an element of variability, even after full allowance has been made for differing local traditions, varying degrees of skill, conservatism and contact with fresh or foreign ideas. We cannot expect, here or in any comparable performing technique, to uncover rules which would yield infallible results at first sight of a new piece, even for experienced singers working within a single tradition. There are bound to be equally acceptable alternatives, just as there are for an editor who realises a figured bass — and the figured bass is an appropriate analogy, because an impromptu realisation is likely to incur discussion and mutual adjustment between players in rehearsal. What is supplied here is but one possible way of performing a piece, by a means which is consistent within itself as far possible.

The preceding pages have concerned themselves largely with the addition of accidentals *causa necessitatis*. Any question as to the why or why not of a specific passage or accidental could be met with the reply *causa pulchritudinis*.

APPENDIX I

Not to include detailed analysis of some complete pieces would be to shirk the main issue. Needless to say, the following appendix is not definitive, many other interpretations being available. It represents an attempt to find rational explanations and solutions for as many as possible of the visible and audible facts. But the art of extemporisation does not lend itself to reason, nor its analysis to verbalizing. In the end, instinct may be more reliable. But solutions can become instinctive only through intimate knowledge and much experience.

Few of the explanations offered in these analyses are provable, few can be documented. If the procedures suggested here are speculative, my only defence is the firm belief that at present there is no surer substitute. Until one is found, we have to proceed with the business of editing with what techniques are available.

The music in the following pages is a reprint of the new edition, by kind permission of Armen Carapetyan and my co-editor, Mrs Margaret Bent, with certain revisions necessitated by the purpose of this appendix. The music is the same, but the accidentals written into the manuscript — those printed on the stave — are placed where they occur in the original source. The editorial accidentals are not always the same as those of the edition, the final version of which was produced in collaboration and more conservatively than is appropriate in the present experimental context.

The editorial accidentals given above the stave represent the result of the final stage of the accompanying analysis, after all necessary adjustments have been made: they should be ignored during the preliminary procedures. The pieces are in the performable version, with the exception of bar 50 of No. 16, whose manuscript accidental C♯ needs to be removed and is printed only for the purposes of analysis. The policies of transcription are those of the edition and it is necessary to mention only these:

line changes in the original are shown by dotted bars,

manuscript strokes denoting new sections are shown by bar-lines through the whole score,

manuscript accidentals apply throughout the bar, by editorial decision, or are cancelled, as necessary,

editorial accidentals apply only to the note they are above, and to immediate repetitions of that pitch.

These abbreviations are used:

Tr[iplex] T[enor] Ct [Contratenor]: to avoid confusion with the pitch C and with Ct, the voice name Counter is not shortened.

Pitch letters with superscript numerals refer to the first or second occurrence of the pitch in the bar.

No. 8 Gloria: Aleyn

The piece is in strict English descant style, written in score notation. I shall examine the effect of the manuscript accidentals last. *Stage 1.* The cadences fall primarily on G, with a lesser number on F and A. There being no key-signatures, the cadence on A normally requires recta B♭, and the F cadence needs no alteration: major thirds and sixths precede the cadence chord automatically. The G cadence calls for F♯ and C♯ as leading notes: D cadences occur too infrequently to be included in an assessment. Defining "cadential" as specified (92) we could set up melodic rules such as:

Triplex: sharpen all Fs leading to an obviously cadential G,

Tenor: sharpen all Cs leading to an obviously cadential D,

Counter: sing B♭ before cadential As. Fs leading upward to Gs may need to be sharpened,

All voices should avoid poor melodic intervals by applying recta B♭ and, approaching a cadential A from above, should use B♭.

These rules would account for all necessary cadences in close position (i.e., $\genfrac{}{}{0pt}{}{5}{8}$) and, as an additional benefit, would cover the Triplex G of an extended position ($\genfrac{}{}{0pt}{}{12}{8}$) cadence on C, and the Tenor note of a similar one on D (as in bar 2). An intelligent group of singers could now achieve a performance realising, with major thirds and sixths as required by theorists, cadences in the following bars: 3-4, 5, 6-7, 7-8, 9-10, 12, 13-14, 16-17, 19, 20, 21 (to C), 24, 26, 28, 30, 32, 34, 36, 38 (see below), 40 (see below), 41-42, 44, 46, 48, 49-50, 51, 53, 55-56.

Stage 2. An examination of the counterpoint between the fundamental voices, Tenor and Counter, does not require any changes to be made in the result achieved in stage 1, but clarifies the occasional obscurity. In bars 9 and 54 it is possible to sharpen the Fs in the Counter. Although the counterpoint of top voice and lowest (tenths diminishing to octaves on the perfection) seems to require this, the combination of middle and lowest does not: the Fs should remain natural. In bars 49 and 52 the temporary imperfect fourth and fifth are acceptable as ornaments.

Had any significant difficulties appeared, as will happen when the top voice is added, we would need to examine the effect of written-in accidentals.

Addition of the top voice to the counterpoint of the lower ones reveals a few places requiring attention. In bar 2, for example, the G is natural, forming a minor tenth before the twelfth, although the Tenor C is sharp. In bar 15 the manuscript G♯ conflicts with the recta B♭ of the Counter and cannot be allowed. At this stage, then, we introduce the written-in chromaticism and examine the texture as a whole. The analytical notes are placed under the relevant bars of the music, and are identified by bar number.

8. Gloria

Ff. 5v - 6 **Aleyn**

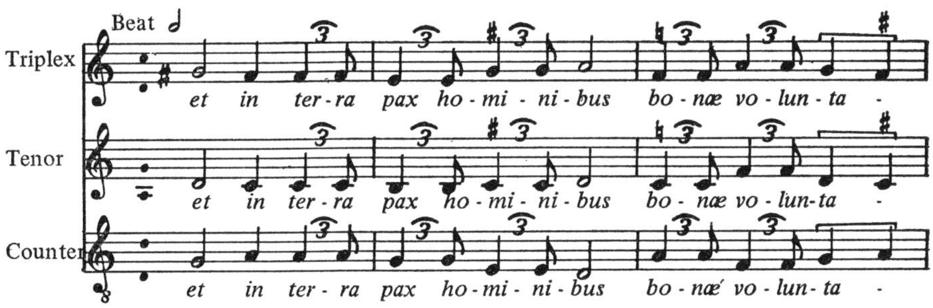

1-2. Tr F♯ preplaced: no space for it in normal position, and it is also cramped as it stands. An afterthought? Perhaps to suggest a move sharpwards to give G♯-A, which might otherwise be interpreted as G-A in a normal close position Phrygian cadence: this corrects the progression in bar 2, where the T C is already sharp by rule. In the melodic progression G-F-E the middle note would not normally be sharpened. The Fs on *terra* are sharp by immediate repetition.

Augmented 4th between Tr and T in 1 could be remedied by C♯ (otherwise mi against fa on a 4th between non-fundamental parts), but melodic line of T would suggest C♮. False relation between G and G♯ is tolerable.

3. Precautionary naturals.

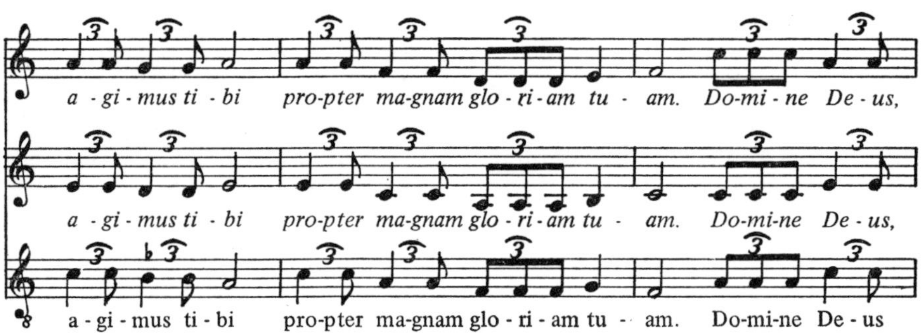

8-9. unavoidable indirect tritone in Tr. If the B has been flattened by melodic rules in stage 1 it will have to be adjusted again. The performer will have to memorise this failure to apply melodic rules.

15. See notes on this passage in the new edition, vol. III. The Tr G♯ prohibits a recta B♭ in the Counter, but neither this, nor the necessary D♯ for the T, could be ascertained in advance when singing at sight: the performers would have to memorise these changes.

18. Counter: unnecessary emphasis of recta B♭ at new section. There is no reason to interpret it as a signature since there are no subsequent Es which could be flattened by recta. All subsequent Bs could be flattened by normal recta. Since it is possible in score notation for one singer to see accidentals in other voices (see 38), especially when they are prominently placed as this one is, the B♭ may be to remind the Tr not to sharpen, by analogy with bar 15, the Gs on *Domine.*

20. T F♯: see bar 21.

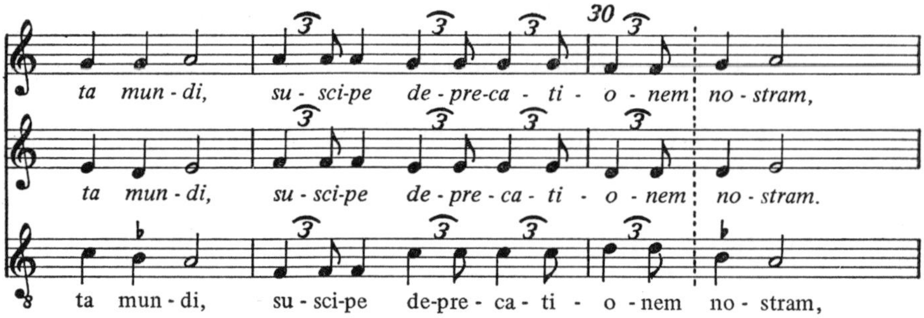

21. T F♯ preplaced in 20. Perhaps the earliest available space for a later addition. It may be required because the G of 21 is not an obvious cadential resting-point, nor within the melodic rules of stage 1.

21-22. Tr: reason for preplacing the F♯ is not clear. Its purpose, as in bar 1, may be to ensure the third degree sharp on G, giving a sharp cadence to A. It is not clear how the T might be aware of the impending sharp cadence. In the Counter, however, there is a new line without a B♭, by contrast with the unnecessary flat in 18: is the distinction significant, to suggest a non-recta cadence to A?

24. Preplaced B♭ in Counter: there is space closer but not immediately before the note. Reason for its appearance not known.

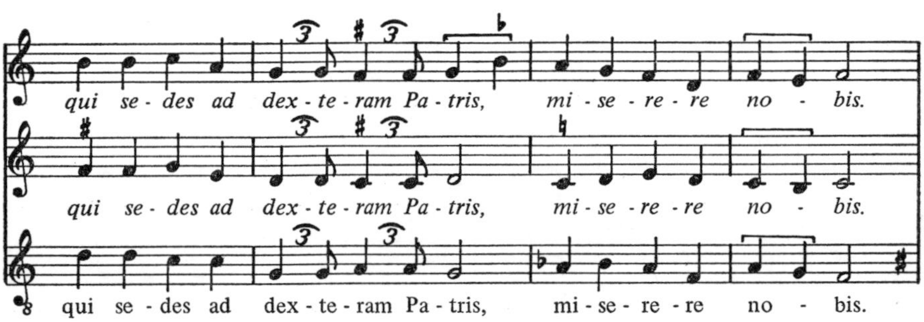

31. T F♯ before this C cadence is not covered by rule and could be omitted: the cadence is not strong.

33. Counter B♭ preplaced for mensural grouping?

34. Counter B♮ preplaced before MS stroke: to imply that B♭ recta is no longer available. Reason for preplacing not clear, but see 38.

35. Reason for preplacing Tr F♯ not known. Visual accidental not needed in lower returning note context. Perhaps it prohibits recta B♭ in 37, thus virtually entailing a sharp cadence to A in 38.

38. Sharp cadence to A may also be suggested by the Counter B♯ of 34, which prohibits B♭ recta. It is not clear how the T learns of this non-Phrygian cadence in time to add F♯ and D♯ in 37 and 38: perhaps it takes the clear visual hint of the B♯ from the Counter in 34 (cf. 18). This cadence was made Phrygian in the edition, despite these hints, on the justifiable grounds that the reasoning is too speculative, and that recta should be preferred.

39. Counter B♭ preplaced at new line. Perhaps to counteract the B♯ of 34 and reinstating both B♮ and B♭ as recta, rather than implying a B♭ signature with E♭ recta: no subsequent E♭s in any case.

40. F and C, if sharpened in stage 1, must be returned to their natural state because cadence to G is too weak. The performers would memorise this, if not musically obvious from the following phrase, which emphasises F♮s. Tr has a recta B♭ causing imperfect fifth off the beat and closing to a third, not between fundamental voices and not in a cadential situation. To the singer it would appear like a Phrygian cadence to A.

47. Tr B♭ because of impending cadence to A.
52. Tr has no hint that G is to be sharpened: T C is already so by stage 1 rule.

Summary

Out of 44 editorial accidentals 12 are recta, applied in places covered by rule or otherwise obvious. 31 are ficta, applied quite normally at cadences to expand the fifth and third: most of these are included in the melodic rules governing the singer, a few are extensions of those rules. Only 1 (bar 37) is not at a cadence.

The simple nature of descant style makes the addition of editorial accidentals relatively simple. I shall now analyse a chanson style piece, modifying the procedures to some extent. No. 16 was chosen because it has several difficult passages, and because it has key-signatures: the number of accidentals in the piece is very small, although one of them raises some possibilities for interesting speculation.

No. 16 Gloria: Roy Henry

This chanson style piece is written in *cantus collateralis* and has a typical contratenor of the French kind, that part being inessential and constructed without much concern for the beauty of its melodic line.

Stage 1. The cadences fall primarily on C and F. We might then set up three melodic rules:

a) sharpen leading notes to C and F cadences (gives B♮ and E♮ in Triplex, F♯ and B♮ in Contratenor, etc.),

b) correct melodic intervals where possible by recta,

c) use recta notes leading downwards to cadential points (gives E♭-D and B♭-A in Tr; B♭-A, E♭-D, A♭-G in T and Ct).

These rules will be referred to by the relevant letter in the subsequent analysis.

Stage 2. All the notes of this stage are under the relevant bars of the music. Italic print represents an examination of the counterpoint of fundamental voices, Triplex and Tenor, where this is necessary: sections in normal type refer to the subsequent examination of the whole texture, including Ct. In doing the analysis it is preferable to proceed horizontally, working through Tr and T complete before passing to the whole texture. A bar by bar vertical examination would fail to account for the melodic emphasis of the music.

16. Gloria

Ff. 12v - 13

Roy Henry

1. *Tr E♭ (c).*
3. *Tr Cs not recognisably a cadence/ T E♮ (a).* Ct B♮ with T E♮ sounds wrong: prefer unaltered version.

5. Ct A^1 and Tr D make A^2 preferably recta ♮: failure to apply rule (c).
6. *Tr recta E♭ optional.* Ct makes it obligatory.
7. *Tr B^1 could be ♮ (a).* With Ct prefer recta ♭.

10. *T E♮ (a).* With Ct E♭ the Tr A♮ is brief and inessential: the augmented interval may be kept. End of bar: as with bar 3, preferable to keep unaltered version, breaking rule (a).

13-14. *all Tr Es could be recta ♮ (a) : E^1 in 14 better as recta ♭, making E in 13 preferably* ♭. Ct E♭ in 14 obligates latter course. Ct in 14 B♮ (a).

17-18. *Tr recta E♭ optional.* Ct MS ficta E♮ obligates Tr E♮ in 17 and probably in 18. Ct cautionary ♭ in 18.

21. Ct B♮ (a).

23. *Tr recta E♭ because of T.*

24. *Tr G not strong enough for cadence, E♭ optional.* Ct B not ♮ if Tr F not ♯: failure to apply rule (a).

25. *Tr B♮ (a).* Ct F♯ (a): reason for reiteration of E♭ of signature is not clear. Just possibly it suggests that the F, and the Tr B by analogy, are not to be sharpened.

27. Ct E♭ obligates recta E♭ in Tr, perhaps entailing —
28. Tr E^1 as recta ♭, which entails T recta A♭. Ct B♮ (a).
29-31. Ct & T recta A♭s are possible but require a ficta A♭ in Tr: prefer recta ♮, failing to observe rule (c). Tr in 31 E♭ optional.

32. Ct B♮ (a): false relation so brief would be tolerable (cf. 37).
33. *Tr recta E♭ because of T, and B♮ (a).* Ct F♯ (a).

36. Ct B♮ in MS preplaced for mensural reasons? It is present because the motive is rather unusual for a cadential figure. See notes in OH III.
37. Ct B♮ (a). (Cf. 32).
38. Ct B must be kept recta: failure to apply rule (a).

42. Ct B♮ (a).

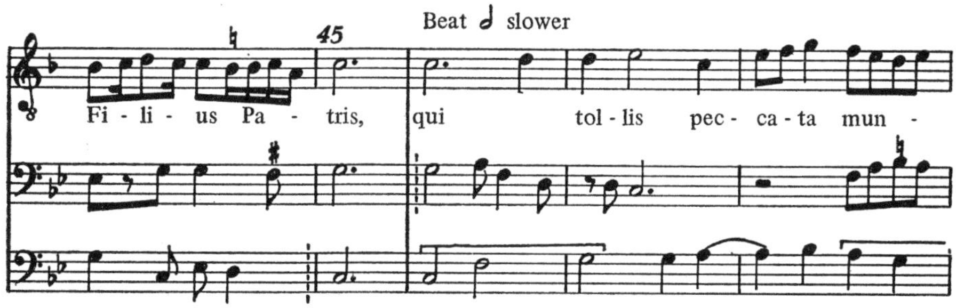

44. *Tr B♮ (a).* Ct F♯ (a).
48. Ct B♮ (a).

50. *Tr ficta C♯ not compatible with recta E♭ (apparently unnecessary) in T. Prefer recta, deleting MS C♯. Reason for preplacing T E♭ not known. An extreme solution accounting for C♯ and unnecessary E♭ might be: T E♭ suggests a flatward shift, giving hexachords on B♭ E♭ A♭ with D♭ recta for following note; Tr C♯ means mi with fa a semitone above, giving D♭ for following note.* In this solution only, the Ct As would be ♭ by recta. The following bar could return to the normal system, but the tonal wrenches are somewhat violent.
52. *Tr E♭ because of T; B♮ (a), with tolerable brief augmented 5th.* Ct F♯ (a).

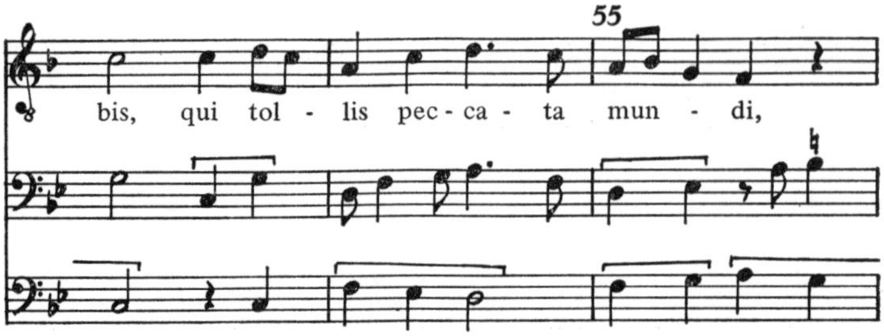

55. Ct B♮ (a).

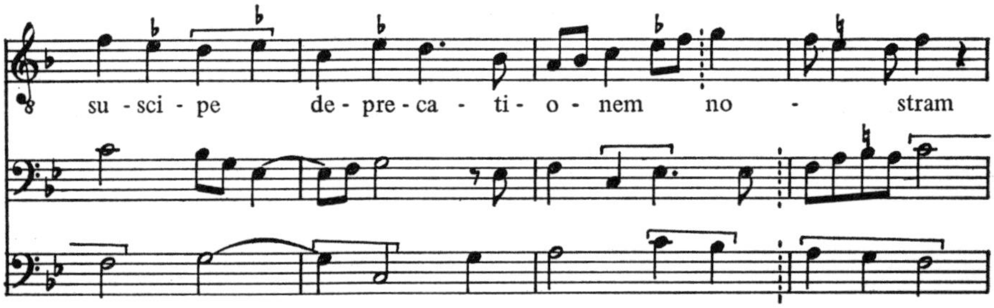

56-57. *Tr E^1 preferably recta ♭ (c), entailing same for E^2 and in 57.* Ct E♭ obligates Tr E♭s. In 57 that the Ct G is not a cadence note is shown by the other parts: failure to observe rule (a).

57-58. Ct Es do not lead to definite cadential Fs: do not make ♮ and ficta. The E♭ in 58 obligates the Tr E♭.

59. Ct B♮ (a).

60-61. *Tr recta E♭s because of T/ T in 61 must then have recta A♭.* Ct B♮ (a) in 61, requiring Tr E^2 to be recta ♮; Tr cadence is hidden at this point.

62. Ct ficta E♮ because of harmonic context.

63. T recta A♭ because of situation in 64.

64. *Tr E^2 must be recta ♭ because of T. E^1 should also be, for aural reasons, entailing recta A♭ in T. Tr B♮ (a), preplaced for mensural reasons? Reason for writing it not known.* Ct obligates recta E♭ in Tr and thus T A♭. Ct F♯ (a).

67. Ct B remains ♭ and recta because of proximity of Tr B♭.

68-69. *Tr E♭s optional, but would entail T recta A♭.* With Ct Tr E♭s preferable. Ct in 69 recta A♭ because of T, entailing B♭ to C: failure to apply rule (a), avoiding false relation with Tr. See 70-73.

70. *Tr recta E♭ because of T: cautionary A♮.*

71. *T recta A♭ (b).*

73. *Tr E♭ because of T. B♮ (a).*

70-73. With the addition of Ct this passage becomes very problematic: the solution here is an attempt to preserve recta where possible. In 71 the T A♭ entails Ct A♭ and thus Tr E♭. Because of situation in 73 preserve recta A♭ and E♭ in 72, except for Ct A^1. In 73, Ct, the choice between E♭-A♮-G-F♯ and E♭-A♭-G-F♯ is open: the sound of the whole makes the latter preferable. Ct F♯ (a).

76. Ct B♮ (a), written in because of tritone?
77. *Tr E♭ because of following T.*
78. *Tr B♮ (a).* Ct F♯ (a).

79. *Tr E♮s, but cadential feeling very weak.* In 79-80 prefer recta A♭s in Ct; Ct E♭ obligates Tr E♭s.
80. *Tr E♭ because of T: B♮ (a).* Ct F♯ (a), despite chromatic progression.
82. *Tr E♭ because of T: B♮ (a), preplaced for mensural reasons, but reason for writing it not known (section 62)* Ct F♯ (a) reason for writing it not known.

Summary

Of the 81 accidentals which appear in the modern transcription, 74 are editorial. Of these, 49 are recta, mostly occurring in places easily recognisable by rule or musicianship; a few would have to be memorised by the performer. 29 of the ficta additions are in $^{6-8}_{3-5}$ cadences, usually obvious; only three could not be applied by rule, and of these, two are marked in the MS (bars 17, 50, 62). Uncertainty about the F cadences without sharpened leading notes in bars 3-4 and 10-11 may be allayed by the numerous times the cadence appears later and cannot be 'corrected' (32, 37-38, 38-39, 40-41, 55, 57-58, 59-60, 69-70, 72).

APPENDIX II: ODD KEY-SIGNATURES, THE CONTRATENOR, TRANSPOSITION, AND INSTRUMENTAL PARTICIPATION

The following appendix represents, frankly, an afterthought which could not be worked into the body of the study without considerable revision, covering, as it does, features of key-signatures, contratenor and transposition, as well as introducing a problem which had seemed very distantly related, if at all, to chromaticism — the question of instrumental participation.

Non-standard signatures such as E♭ alone I have discovered primarily in contratenor parts, hardly ever in fundamental voices. In sections 65-66 I discuss the possibility that some contratenors were not subject to the hexachord and solmization system as the other voices were: naturally, a signature of E♭ cannot 'deliver' a normal series of hexachords at any transposition. The signature may be to ensure that the low B♮ does not lose recta status. Whatever the signature, Beb, eb or e, the Bs at both octave levels usually need to be constantly flattened: the low B♭s will, under the signature e (E♭ alone) be ficta flats. We have seen the medieval aversion to such ficta notes (55-57, *passim*). Can this situation be avoided? We can add an editorial B♭ to the signature, but this is certainly an unwarranted interference in order to 'correct' something we do not understand, although the remedy may be necessary as a temporary expedient. Without adding to the music already written in the source, we can legitimize the E♭ signature only by transposing the whole voice up a fifth, producing a single B♭ as signature: under the theory proposed this would transpose the gamut, replacing the low ficta B♭s originally required almost throughout the voice with F♮s, but these would logically still be ficta. The original low ficta B♭ is singable but, being ficta, the note may not have been physically present on a fifteenth century instrument. The ficta F♮ produced by the transposition in place of the non-existent B♭, being recta in normal situations, would certainly exist on any instrument. The F♯ produced by the original recta B♮ would be recta in the transposed version: that note may not exist on the instrument, it is true, but since the recta B♮ normally needs flattening, its transposition, the F♯, will not be needed.

Playing the contratenor, in which these odd signatures mainly occur, on an instrument would emancipate the voice from dependence on solmization, a purely vocal technique. This may be the first stylistic evidence (other than the rare markings such as *trompetta*) for instrumental performance of contratenor parts. The low B♭ does not appear in the signature for the very practical reason that the note does not exist on the instrument performing the contratenor: on keyboard instruments with incomplete lower octaves notes are physically unobtainable in the low registers.[25a] By the same reasoning, the presence of low B♭ in the signature of tenor, or as an accidental in that voice, might indicate vocal performance. But such contratenors would have to be put up a fifth, entailing transposition of the whole texture.

Transposition by such an interval, here indicated by an oddity in the signature of one part, need be no surprise. Transposition in the sixteenth century was shown by certain clef arrangements, the *chiavette* technique. Several medieval pieces are known in two sources, one of which has the music transposed a fifth[26]: in order to make Damett's paired Gloria and Credo in Old Hall identical in pitch-level, the latter has to be sung a fifth higher (see my article "Mass Pairs..." in *Revue Belge de Musicologie* XIX (1965), p. 22).

Why might such a technique have been used, when the simpler procedure would be to write the music at the pitch required? The effect of such a shift on the other parts of the piece is as follows: with signatures conflicting –,e,eb the version a fifth higher produces ♯,b,b(f♮) with hexachords on D, G, C and C, F, B♭ for fundamental voices, and an assumption that contratenor is not dependent on hexachord principles. Sharp signatures did not exist in the Middle Ages and therefore could not be written (25, 27, 37, 55). Transposition may be yet another way of using in practice and performance things which were not acceptable in theory or in visible form.

The same hypothesis does not explain transposition for signatures such as b,e,eb or b,eb,Beb whose versions at the higher pitch are (f♮),b,b(f♮) and (f♮),b(f♮),(F♮)b(f♮). As –,♭,♭ these two signatures

25a. Ann Scott independently proposes a very similar argument in "The performance of the Old Hall descant settings", *Musical Quarterly* 56 (1970) pp. 14-26.

26. See for example Nos 19 & 56 of "The Worcester Fragments", ed. L. Dittmer, American Institute of Musicology, Rome 1957, pp.29 & 95: also, from the time contemporary with Old Hall, the chanson *La belle se sit* by Dufay (see Charles Hamm, "A Chronology of the works of Guillaume Dufay", Princeton University Press 1964, pp. 32-33).

are acceptable. But the ficta required, which would involve accidentals one degree farther sharpwards, may have been more extreme than was preferred. It is also possible that, on a participating instrument, just as the low ficta B♭ was absent, extreme sharps may have been missing.

There are many aspects which still need to be studied. In particular, statistical evidence is required, for example, to discover whether odd signatures occur only in, or predominate in, contratenor parts. We must heed Lowinsky's warning, already noted, about drawing conclusions from relatively few examples. There is no justification for premature assertions. But the publication of ideas and interesting coincidences from a few sources can indicate what we should search for in a wider repertory. At that time, we must beware of noting *only* those features which tend to confirm ideas only tentatively expressed.

APPENDIX III

OH MS ACCIDENTALS

These are indicated as follows: folio number (bold, and always at the left hand edge);

stave (small roman numeral. Where a number of staves have the same signature, or what appears to be a signature, these are noted first — reading the accidentals upwards on the stave — and accidentals within the body of each stave are itemised later);

number of the note on the stave (rests are not counted, ligatures are counted as a single note. Normally, the accidental stands before the note referred to, but when an asterisk is given the accidental stands above or below the note);

Pitch and symbol of accidental (an unqualified ♯ or ♭ refers to f♯ or b♭. ♯ covers all variant forms, including ♮, since these are usually graphically indistinguishable. Variant forms of ♭, e.g., c, f, g, are distinguished. The octave of the given pitch is shown only where ambiguous).

Entries on the same MS stave are separated by ; , those on different staves by / . The following abbreviations occur:

er for erased,

rd for red.

1v. iv.1* ♯ / vii.8 ♯ / viii.9 c♯ / x.17 ♯ / xi.18 c♯ / xii.5 ♭

2. vi.13 ♭ / vii.16 ♯ / xii.7 ♭

2v. iv.25 ♯ ; 28 f♭ ; 33 ♯

3. vi.31 ♭ / xii.30 ♯

4. iii.1 ♭ / iv.10* ♭ ; 12 ♯ / v.9 c♯ / vi.1 ♭ / vii.15 b♯ ; 17 ♯ ; 18 ♯ er / ix.1 ♭ ; 27 ♭ / xi.15* ♭ ; 17 b♯ / xii.1 ♭

4v. i.26 ♯ / ii.3 ♯ ; 27 c♯ ; 28 rd c♯ er ; 30 rd c / iii.2 c♯ / v.1 c♯ ; 7 c / vii.1 ♯ ; 17 ♯ ; 29 c♯ / x.9 c♯

5. i.19 ♯ / ii.1 g♯ / iv.6 ♭ / v.9 c♯ / vi.1 ♭ ; 12 b♯ ; 25 ♭ / ix.1 ♭

5v. i.11 ♭ / iv.1 ♯ / vii.31 g♯ / x.33 ♯ / xi.21 ♯ / xii.10 ♭

6. iii.10 ♭ / iv.23 ♯ / vi.12 ♭ ; before MS stroke b♯ / ix.1* ♭

6v. i.7 ♯ ; 20 f ; 36 ♯ ; 40 f / iii.1 ♭ ; 17* ♭ / iv.31 ♯ / v.15 ♭ ; 36 b♯ / vi.1 ♭ / vii.14 c♯ ; 39 ♯ ; 48 ♭ / viii.7 ♭ ; 31 b♯ / ix.16 ♭ / x.1 ♯ ; 5 c♯ ; 11 f ; 26 ♯ / xi.6 ♭ ; 14 b♯ / xii.13 c♯ ; 17 c

7. i.24 ♯ ; 38 f / ii.10 c♯ ; 12 c ; 33 ♭ ; 36 b♯ / iii.1 ♭ ; 20 b♯ ; 29 ♭ / iv.9 ♯ ; 33 f / vi.9 ♭ / vii.1 ♯ ; 10 ♭ ; 21 f ; 28 ♯ ; 37 c♯ ; 52 f / ix.4 ♭ ; 16 b♯

7v. i.28 ♯ / vii.7 ♯ ; 16 ♯ / viii.5 b♯ er / ix.1 ♯ er ; 17 ♭ ; 27 b♯ / x.21 ♯ ; 29 f ; 43 ♭ / xii.30 ♭

8. ii.29 ♯ / iii.20 ♭ / iv.29 ♭ / v.24 c♯ ; 31 ♭ / vi.14 ♭ / viii.1 ♭ ; 6 c♯ ; 12 ♯ / ix.16 ♭

8v. i.7* ♯ ; 16* f / iii.11 ♭ / iv.5 b♯ / vi.4 ♭ ; 7 b♯ ; 10 ♭ / vii.45 ♭ / ix.15 ♭ / x.21*b♯ / xii.1 ♭ ; 12 b♯ er ; 17 b♯ ; 29 ♭

9. i.38 ♯ ; 49 ♭ / ii.33 c♯ / iii.26 ♭ / iv.15 b♯ / vii.17 ♭ / x.21 b♯

9v. sigs: i-iv-vii-x.1 ♭, ii-v-viii-xi.1 e♭,♭, iii-vi-ix-xii.1 ♭,e♭,♭ / i.19 e♭ / iii.24 e♭ / x.1 e♭ (above sig) ; 33* b♯

10. sigs: i-iv-vii-x.1 ♭, ii-v-vii-xi.1 e♭,♭, iii-vi-ix-xii.1♭, e♭, ♭

10v. sigs: i-vi-ix-xii.1 ♭, ii.1 e♭,♭, iii.1 ♭,e♭,♭ / ii.20 e♭,♭ / vi.24 ♭ / vii.5 c♯ / ix.19 ♭ / x.13 c♯ ; 15 ♯ er ; 37* c♯ ; 43 ♭ / xi.25 c♯ ; 27 g♯ / xii.24 ♭

11. sigs: iii-vi-ix-xii.1 ♭ / i.10* c♯ / vi.31 ♭ / vii.13 ♯ / xi.21 c♯

11v. sigs: iii.1 ♭ / i.17 c♯ / ii.11 g♯ ; 23 (er version) rd g♯ er / iv.17 ♯ ; 45 ♯ / v.12 ♯ ; 19 c♯ / vi.1 ♯ ; 12 f / viii.32 ♭

12. vii.2 ♭ / ix.1 ♭ ; 7 b♯

12v. sigs: iii to x.1 ♭ / vi.1 c♯ / vii.28* b♯ / x.10 b♯

13. sigs: i to xii.1 e♭,♭ / ii.8 e♯ ; 26 e♭ / iii.19 b♯ / vi.16 b♯ / vii.6 ♯ / x.7 e♭

13v. ii.24 ♭ / iii.8 ♭ ; 37 ♯ / vii.2 ♭ ; 7 b♯ ; 30 ♭ / viii.1 ♭ / x.5 ♭ ; 14 ♯ ; 33 b♯ / xi.2 rd ♭ ; 18 rd b♯ ; 27 rd ♭ / xii.1 ♯

14. sigs: i to xii.1 ♭ / iv.25 b♯ / v.24 ♭ / viii.1 e♯ (above sig) / ix.9 b♯ ; 27 ♭

15. i.20* ♯ / ix.26 ♯ / x.7 ♯ / xii.1 ♭

15v. vii.14* ♭ ; 17 b♯ / ix.14 ♭

16v. sigs: i to x.1 ♭ / i.7 c♯ ; 16 b♯ / iii.36* c♯ / vi.26 b♯ / ix.13 ♯ ; 16 f ; 27 b♯

17. sigs: i to iv.1 ♭, v to viii.1 e♭, ix to xii.1 e♭,♭

17v. iv.26 ♯

18. x.26 ♭ ; 35 b♯

18v. sigs: x to xii.1 ♭ / i.14 ♯ ; 17 f♭ / ii.14 ♯ / ix.2 ♭

19. sigs: vii to xii.1 ♭ / i.7 c♯ / ii.7 ♭ / iii.22 ♯ / vi.49 ♭ ; 53 b♯ / vii.18 b♯ / ix.2 ♭ / xii.33 b♯

19v. sigs: iii to x.1 ♭

20. sigs: i to xii.1 ♭,e♭,♭ / ii.18 e♯ / iv.27 e♯ ; 30 e♭ ; 41 e♯ ; 43 e♭ / vi.19 b♯ / viii.17 e♯

20v. i.24 ♭ / ii.8 ♭ / iii.21 ♯ / iv.13 ♯ / v.17 ♭ / vi.34 ♭ ; 37* ♭ / vii.12 ♯ ; 24 ♯ / viii.11 ♯

21. sigs: viii to xi.1 ♭ / i.1 ♯ ; 21* ♭ / ii.1 ♭ / iii.3 ♯ ; 35* ♭ / v.9 ♯ / vii.13 ♭ ; 29 e♭ / viii.2 c♯ / ix.4 b♯ ; 8* ♭ / x.23 e♭ / xi.4 b♯

21v. i.27 g♯ / ii.15 g♯/ iii.4 ♯ / vi.9 ♯ / viii.20 ♯ / ix.27 g♯

22. i.33 c♯ / ii.19 g♯ / iii.1 g♯ ; 16* c♯ / v.9 c♯ / vi.8 c♯ / viii.20 ♯ / xi.2 c♯

22v. sigs: viii to xi.1 ♭ / iv.15 ♯ / viii.4 b♯ ; 10 ♭

23. sigs: ix to xi.1 ♭ / iv.10 ♭ / xi.5* b♯

23v. i.18 ♭ / iv.1 ♯ ; 16 ♭ / v.7 c♯ / vi.17 ♯ / vii.25 ♯ / x.4 ♯ / xi.12 c♯ / xii.1 ♭

24. ii.14 ♯ / iii.5 ♭ / iv.35 ♯ / v.19 ♭/vi.24 ♭/vii.27 ♭/viii.1 ♭;14 rd ♯ / ix.2 rd ♭ ; 7 c♯ / x.38 ♯ / xi.1 ♭

24v. i.28 g♯ / iii.29 c♯

25. ii.22 c♯ / iv.14 ♯ ; 20 c♯

25v. ix.1 ♭ ; 19 ♭ / x.1 ♭

27. sigs: vii to xi.1 ♭ / ix.1* b♯ ; 9 ♭

27v. v.14 c♯ / vii.1 ♯ / viii.4 c♯ / ix.28 ♯ / x.49 c♯

28. i.9* ♯ ; 26 ♯ / iv.17 ♯ / vii.10* ♭ / x.21 ♯

28v. sigs: x to xii.1 ♭ / ii.24 ♭ / iii.15 b♯ / iv.9 ♭ / v.6 ♭ ; 10 ♯ ; 35* ♭ / vi.29 ♯ / vii.12 ♭ ; 17 ♯ / xi.4 b♯ ; 5 e♭

29. iv.25 ♯ / vii.9 c♯

29v. i.14 c♯ ; 15 ♯ / ii.8 ♯ / iii.19 ♯ ; 42 c♯ / iv.41 g♯ / v.30* c♯ ; 42 g♯ / vii.13 c♯

30. i.10 ♯ / iii.7 ♯ / iv.13 ♯ / v.22 g♯ ; 30 ♯ / vi.11 c♯ / vii.6 g♯ ; 13 c♯ ; 15 g♯ / viii.8 c♯ ; 17 ♯ / x.7* ♭ / xi.1 c♯ ; 30 g♯

30v. i.7 ♯ ; 9 f♭ (e♭ er) ; 27* ♯ / iii.1 ♭ ; 29 ♯ ; 32 c♯ ; 33 ♭ / iv.30 ♯ / v.10 ♭ / vi.2 ♯ / vii.4 c♯ ; 30* ♯ / viii.9* ♯ ; 21 f♭ / ix.12 ♯ ; 26 c♯ / x.7 ♯ / xii.13 ♯

31. sigs: v to xii.1 ♭ / i.5 ♯ / iii.35* ♭ / iv.1 c♯ / v.23 c♯ / vi.12 ♯ ; 24* c♯ ; 26 b♯ / vii.9 b♯ ; 10 ♭

31v. sigs: i to viii.1 ♭ / i.23 e♯ / iii.50 e♭ / v.25 e♭

32. sigs: i to xi.1 ♭,e♭,♭

32v. i.15 e♭ ; 30 ♭ / ii.1* c♯ ; 25 c♯ ; 34 ♯ / iii.9 c♯ ; 37 ♯ ; 43 f / iv.4 ♯ / vi.2 ♯ ; 24* ♭ / vii.55 c♯ / viii.7 c♯ / x.9 ♭ ; 28 b♯ / xi.9 ♭

33. i.46 g♯ / ii.13 c♯ / iii.1 c♯ ; 4 c ; 35* ♯ / iv.6 ♯ ; 17 ♯ half er ; 23 ♯ / vi.12♭; 15 b♯

33v. sigs: i to xi.1 ♭ / ii.19 e♭ / iii.43 e♭ / iv.15 e♭ ; 27 e♯ / vii.3 e♭ ; 28 e♭ ; 35 e♯ / viii.16* e♭ / x.3 e♭ ; 13 e♯ ; 25 e♭ / xi.11 e♭

34. sigs: i to v.1 ♭ er, e♭,♭, vi to xi.1♭,e♭,♭ / i.5 b♯; 7 ♭ / iv.45* ♭

34v. i.9 c♯ ; 15 ♭ ; 19 b♯ ; 30 ♯ ; 43 f / iii.52 c♯ / iv.14 ♯ ; 15 ♯ er / vi.15 ♯ ; 24 f ; 34 c♯ / viii.20 ♯

35. i.1 ♭ / v.31 ♭ / vi.2 ♯ / vii.27 ♭ ; 30 e♭ ; 35 e♯ / viii.25* ♭ ; 27 b♯ / ix.7 ♭ / x.15 ♭ / xi.7 ♭ ; 11 b♯

35v. i.22 ♯ / vii.27 ♯ / xi.14 c♯

36. sigs: v-viii-xi.1 ♭ / vi.10 ♭ / ix.14 ♭ / xii.26 ♭

36v. sigs: iii-vi-ix-xii.1 ♭ / i.15 ♭ ; 23 b♯ / iv.14* c♯ / vii.4 ♭ / ix.3 b♯ ; 5 ♭ / x.20 ♭

37. vi.22 ♭ / ix.1 ♭ ; 23 b♯

38. iii.17 ♭

38v. iv.2 ♯ ; 32 f / ix.17 ♭ / x.6 ♯ ; 12 f / xii.1 ♭

39. sigs: iii-vi.1 ♭ ; *Ave* after clef & ix.1 ♭ / *Ave* iv.8 c♯ / vii.8* c♯ ; 33 ♯ er ; 37 ♯ / viii.5 c♯ / xii.14 ♭ ; 17 ♭

39v. i.1 ♯ ; 18 f / ii.35 c♯ / iii.7 ♭ ; 19 ♭ / iv.8 ♯ / ix.22 ♭ / x.20 ♯ / xii.1 ♭

40. sigs: iii-vi-viii-ix-xi-xii.1 ♭ / x.13 ♭

40v. i.2 g♯ ; 4 ♯ ; 8 c♯ ; 15 ♯ / ii.2 d♯ ; 4 c♯ / iii.4 ♭ / iv.2 c♯ ; 6* ♯ / v.2 g♯ ; 5* g ; 6* c♯ ; 11 g♯ ; 19 c♯ ; 21 c / vii.5 c♯ ; 16 ♯

41. ix.8* ♭ ; 17 b♯ / xii.15 ♭ ; 22 b♯

41v. i.33 ♯ / iv.10 ♯

44. vii.34 ♯

44v. iv.38 ♯

45. x.3 c♯

45v. ix.6 ♭ ; 30 ♭ ; 35 b♯

46. iii.11 ♭ / iv.32 ♯ / vi.12 ♭ / vii.35 ♯

47v. vi.19 ♭

48. vi.29 ♭ / xii.16 ♭

48v. iii.1 ♭ er ; 20 b♯

49. ii.24* ♭; 25* d♭ er (intended as b♭: 3 notes written 3rd too high and er, ♭ with them) / iii.23 ♭ / vi.2 ♭ ; 11 b♯ ; 22 ♭ / x.4 ♯ ; 13 f

49v. vi.15* ♭ / ix.1 ♭ ; 6 b♯ ; 9 ♭ / x.35 ♯ / xii.17 ♭ ; 29 b♯

50. iii.1 ♭ / iv.27 ♯ / x.9 ♯

50v. i.6 ♯ / iv.2 c♯ ; 12 ♯ / vii.19 ♯ ; 31 c♯ / x.3 ♯ / xii.19 ♭

51. i.1 ♯ / vii.3 ♯

51v. i.1 ♯ / iv.1 ♯ / vii.21 ♯

52. sigs: ii-iii-v-vi-viii-ix-xi-xii.1 ♭ / iii.1* e♭ / iv.17* ♭ ; 32 b♯ / vii.33 ♭ ; 43 b♯

52v. i.1 ♭

54. i.3 ♯ / ii.17* b♯ er / iv.31 ♯

54v. i.25 b♯ / iv.31 ♯ ; 38 f / vi.32 ♭

55. iii.13 ♭ ; 32 b♯ er / 35 ♭

55v. i.2 ♯ / iv.11 b♯

56. ii.9 ♯ ; 21 f ; 44 ♯ / iii.1 ♯ ; 36 ♯ ; 40 f / v.12 c♯ / vi.9 ♯ ; 37 ♯ / ix.5 c♯ / xii.1 ♯

56v. iii.7 ♯ ; 21 f

57v. sigs: iv to vii.1 ♭ / i.22 ♭ / ii.10 ♭ / v.31 b♯ / vii.6 ♯

58v. ii.28 ♯ / iii.21 ♯ / ix.7 ♯

59. i.28*♯/ ii.29 f ; 31* c♯ / iii.23* ♯ ; 44 c♯ / v.34 ♯ / vii.14* ♯ / xiii.6 ♭ ; 11* b♯

59v. vii.10 ♯ / viii.25 ♯

60. sigs: i to x.1 ♭ / i.17 b♯ / ii.1 c♯ / iv.6 ♯ ;8 b♯; 10 ♭/ viii.10 e♭

60v. i.24* ♭ / ii.34 ♭ ; 38 b♯ / viii.16 ♭

61. sigs: i to xi.1 ♭

61v. ii.18 c♯ / iv.45 ♯ / vii.8 ♯

62. sigs: ii to viii, x to xiii.1 ♭ / iii.30 ♯ ; 32 f / iv.51* b♯ / v.2* b♯ ; 24 ♭ ; 36 ♯ ; 39 f / viii.5* high ♯ / x.6 b♯

62v. iii.16 rd c♯ / v.18* blue c♯ ; 28 blue a♭ (placed high, and may be b♭) / vi.24 blue c♯ / vii.25 g♯ ; 38 rd c♯ / ix.16 ♯ ; 37 c♯

63. ii.18 rd ♭ ; 24 b♯ / iv.23 g♯ / v.20 c♯ ; 21 c / vi.18 rd ♯ / viii.13 ♭ / ix.6 ♭ ; 18 b♯ / x.9 ♭ ; 18 b♯ / xi.1 rd ♭ ; 12 ♭ / xii.1 c♯

63v. i.25 c♯ / vii.45 ♭ / viii.1 ♭ ; 29 c♯ / ix.18 ♭ / xii.31 c♯

64. sigs: vii to xi.1 ♭ / iii.14 ♭ / iv.9 ♭ / vi.1 ♯ / ix.8* b♯ ; 24 rd ♭ / x.13 ♭ er ; 14 e♭ er / xii.8 c♯

64v. sigs: iv to xii.1 ♭ / i.22 b♯ / ii.18 b♯ / iii.10 b♯ ; 23 ♯ / viii.32 b♯ / ix.14 ♯

65. sigs: i to v.1 ♭, vi-vii.1 d♭ (for e♭),♭, viii to xii.1 e♭,♭ / ii.17 b♯ / iii.18 b♯ / iv.19 ♯ / v.21 ♯ ; 28* c♯ ; 32* b♯ / vii.10 e♯ / x.12 e♭,♭ ; 16 ♯

65v. sigs: *Tenor* after clef & x to xii.1 ♭ / iii.1 ♯ / iv.3♯ / vii.16* ♯ / x.12 b♯ / xi.14 b♯

66. i.34 ♯ / ii.27 ♯ / v.21 ♯ / viii.27 ♯ / ix.8 ♭ / xii.5 ♭ ; 11 b♯

66v. vi.3 ♯ ; 42 ♭

67. sigs: i to xiv.1 ♭ / ix.18* rd e♭

68v. i.18 ♭ / ii.21 g♯ / iii.21 g♯ / iv.48* ♭ / v.38* ♭ / vi.5* g♯ ;

37 ♯ / viii.44* rd ♯ / ix.27* rd g♯ ; 54 ♯ / x.22 ♭ / xi.41 ♭ / xii.7 ♭ ; 17 ♯ ; 51 ♯ ; 51* rd ♭ / xiii.10 rd ♭ ; 46 ♭ / xiv.4 rd ♭

69. sigs: i to vii, ix to xiv.1 ♭ / i.27 ♯ / ii.7 ♯ ; 14 f♭ ; 35* c♯ / iii.9 d♯ / iv.36 ♯ ; 39 b♯ / vi.5* c♯ / vii.21 b♯ / viii.7 ♭ / ix.4* b♯ ; 5* ♯; 10 f♭ / xi.6 b♯; 13 ♭; 16 c♯ ; 22 b♯ / xii.24 b♯

69v. sigs: iv to xii.1 ♭ / iv.37* b♯ / x.6 b♯

70. sigs: i to iv.1 ♭, vi to x.1 e♭, xi.1 e♭,♭, xii.-xiii.1 e♭ / ii.6 ♯ / iv.46 ♯ / v.2 e♭ / xi.56 ♭ / xiii.25 ♭ ; 36 ♯

70v. sigs: i to x,xii.1 ♭ / i.18 e♭ / iii.1 e♭ ; 10 ♯ ; 12 e♯ ; 17 f / iv.28 e♭ / v.12 e♭ ; 29 e♭ / vi.28 e♭ ; 39 e♯ / vii.27 e♭ ; 34 e♯ / viii.2 e♭ ; 35 e♯ / ix.4 e♭ / x.1 e♭ / xi.38 e♭

71. sigs: i to xii.1 ♭,e♭,♭ / xi.17 e♯

71v. sigs: i to xii.1 ♭ / i.8* ♯ ; 14 f / iii.16 b♯ ; 28 ♭ / iv.34* b♯ / v.7 b♯ / vii.2 c♯ / viii.25 ♯ ; 27 f / ix.7 e♯ / xi.25 b♯

72. sigs: i to xii.1 & *Tenor* after clef ♭,e♭,♭ / i.2* ♯ ; 6 b♯ ; 14 ♭ ; 20 e♯ ; 37 rd e♭ / ii.5 e♯ / iii.24* e♯ / iv.9 rd ♯ / v.29* rd e♯ / vi.10 e♯ ; 43* b♯ / vii. 40* e♯ / viii.28 e♯ ; 45 e♭ / ix.7 e♯ / x.29 b♯ / xii.16 e♯

72v. sigs: ix to xii.1 ♭ / viii.30 ♯

73. ix.4 ♭ ; 6 b♯

73v. vii.23 ♭ / ix.57 ♭ / xi.25 ♭

74. sigs: ix to xi.1 ♭ / iv.15 ♭

74v. i.16 ♭ / iii.1* ♯ / iv.33 ♯ / v.4 ♯ / vi.20 ♯ / vii.33 ♯ / ix.32 ♯ / x.14 ♭

75. sigs: i to xi.1 ♭

75v. i.24 ♯

76. xi-xii.1 ♭

76v. sigs: ix to xi.1 ♭ / ii.8 ♭ / viii.46* ♭ / ix.21 b♯

77. i.3 ♯ / iv.16 ♯ / ix.7 ♭; 11 b♯; 14 ♭ / x.3 ♭ ; 11 b♯ / xi.6 ♭ / xii.1 ♭

77v. vii.22 ♯ / viii.15* c♯ / x.25 c♯

78. i.1 ♭ ; 6 b♯ / ii.22 c♯ ; 34 c / vi.20* ♭ ; 23 b♯ / vii.1 b♯ ; 35 ♭ / ix.1 ♭ / x.1 ♭

78v. i.27 e♭ / ii.13 ♯ ; 36 c♯ / iv.13 c♯ ; 32 ♯ ; 36 f / v.38 ♯ ; 42 f / vi.15 ♯ / xi.3 ♭ ; 11 b♯ / xii.2* ♭

79. ii.13 b♯ half er ; 32 ♯ / iv.3 c♯ ; 11 c ; 17 g♯ ; 20 c♯ / vi.4 c♯ ; 27 g♯ / vii.1 ♯

79v. ii.20 ♭ / iii.35 ♭ / iv.22 ♭ ; 50 b♯ / vi.11 f♭ ; 24 ♭ ; 26 b♯ / vii.13 ♭ ; 22 b♯ / viii.18* ♭ ; 29* b♯ ; 61 ♭ / ix.36 ♭ / x.31 ♭ / xi.3 ♭

80. sigs: i. to xi.1 ♭

80v. sigs: ii-iii-v-vi-ix-xii.1 ♭ / i.2 ♯ ; 4 ♭ ; 6 ♯ / iii.14 e♭ / iv.7* ♯ / vii.3 ♭

81. sigs: iii-vi-ix-xii.1 ♭ / i.1 ♯ / ii.1 ♭ / iv.3 ♯ / v.8 ♯ / vii.9 ♯ ; 26 g♯ / x.1 ♯ ; 16 f ; 25 ♯ er / xii.16 b♯ er

81v. ii.1 ♭ ; 4 ♯ / iv.18* ♯ ; 24* ♯ / v.14 ♯ / vii.4 ♯ ; 11 f / viii.23 ♯ er ; 26 ♯

82. sigs: iii-vi-ix-xii.1 ♭ / i.21 ♭

82v. i.6 ♯ ; 7 f ; 20 ♯ ; 27 ♭ / iii.1 ♭ / iv.12 c♯ / vii.6 c♯ / x.6 ♯ ; 16 f

83. i.1 ♯ ; 8 f / iv.22 ♯ ; 23 c♯

84. iv.9 ♯ ; 10 f / vii.21 g♯

84v. i.2 ♯ / iv.20 ♯ ; 21 f / v.6 ♭ ; 7 b♯ ; 8 ♭ / viii.6 ♭ / ix.4 ♭ ; 9 ♭ er / x.19 ♯ 1 xi.13 b♯ ; 15 ♭ / xii.13 ♭ ; 23 ♭ er ; 27* e♯ ; 30* a♯ (*sic*, above final note)

85. iii.14 ♭ / vii.1 ♯ / ix.6 ♭ ; 19 ♭ / xii.8 ♭

85v. iv.16 c♯ / vii.11 ♯ ; 19* c♯

86. iv.15 c♯

86v. i.1 ♯ / iii.6 ♭ / iv.5 ♯ / v.8 ♯ ; 9 f / vi.1 ♭ ; 13 ♭ / viii.11 ♯ / ix.1 ♭ ; 2 b♯ ; 6 ♭ / xii.4 ♭ ; 5 c♯ ; 8* ♭

87. sigs: ii-iii-vi-viii-xi.1 ♭ / i.6 ♯ / iii.7 b♯ / v.17 ♭ / vi.7 ♭ / vii.23 ♯ ; 25 c♯ ; 31 f / x.2 ♯
87v. i.16 c♯ / iv.4 ♯ / vii.13* c♯ / x.5 c♯
88. i-vii.1 ♯
88v. x.9 ♯
89. sigs: i-iii-vi-ix-xi-xii.1 ♭ / vii.5 ♯ ; 22* ♭ / xii.9 ♭
89v. i.10* ♯ ; 19 f / ii.18 ♭ / iv.2 ♯ ; 4 f ; 36 ♭ ; 39 b♯ / v.10 ♭ ; 26* b♯ ; 30 ♭ / vi.29 ♭ ; 36* ♯ / vii.3* ♭ ; 8 b♯ ; 33* ♯' viii.19 ♯ ; 33 f / ix.10 ♭ ; 11 b♯ ; 19 ♭
90. sigs: i to viii.1 ♭ / ii.11 ♯ ; 21 f / v.26* e♭
90v. v.44 ♯ / vi.28 ♯ / vii.1 ♭ ; 15 ♯ ; 47 ♭ / ix.18 ♯
91v. vii. 25 c♯
92. i.23 ♭
92v. i.6 ♯ ; 14 f ; 15 c♯ ; 27 ♯ ; 36 f / v.6 ♭ ; 15 b♯ / vi.2 ♭ ; 26 b♯ / ix.12 ♭ / x.1 ♯ ; 11 c♯ / xii.26 ♭ & c♯ ; 27 c
93v. i.1 ♭ / viii.20 c♯ ; 22 g♯
94. iii.32 ♭ ; 33 b♯ / v.17 g♯ & c♯ / vii.45 ♭ / viii.7 ♭ ; 20 b♯ / x.2 ♭ / xii.6 ♭
94v. iii.18 ♭ ; 30 ♯ / vi.7 ♭ / vii.9 ♭
95. iv.7 e♭ / vi.8 e♭ ; 20 ♭ / viii.17 ♭ / ix.1 ♭ ; 24 ♭
96. i.26 ♯
96v. i.28 ♯ / ii.23 ♯ / iv.12 ♯ / vi.6 ♯ / viii.3 ♭ / ix.1 ♭ / x.5 ♭ / xi.1 ♭
97. i.20 ♯ / iii.7* ♯ ; 31 ♯ / v.6 ♯ ; 28 ♭ / vi.9 ♯ / x.1 ♭ ; 8 b♯
97v. vi.1 ♭
98. iii.7 ♭ / vii. *Sanctus* after clef ♯
98v. iii.28 ♭ / ix. *Qui* after clef ♭ / xi.11 c♯
99. i.3 ♭ / ii.1 ♭ ; 11* b♯ / iii.5 ♭
99v. i.16 c♯ / iii.8 ♯ ; 21 ♯ ; 23 f / viii.5 ♭ ; 7 b♯ ; 8 ♭ ; 21 b♯ / ix.1 ♭ ; 3 b♯ ; 4 ♭ ; 17 b♯ / x.15 ♭ ; 16 b♯ ; 19 ♭
100. i.7 ♯ ; 17* f / iii.14 ♯ ; 20 f / iv.29 ♭ / v.12 ♭ ; 14 b♯ / vi.2 ♭ ; 6 b♯ / vii.13 ♭ / viii.1 ♭ / ix.5 ♭ ; 11* b♯ / x.1 ♭ / xi.1 ♭ ; 18 b♯
100v. sigs: vii to ix & xi.1 ♭ / x.6 ♭
101. i.14 ♭ / iii.13 ♭ / iv.8 g♯ ; 16 ♯ / v.5 c♯ vii.28 ♯ / xii.5 ♭
101v. sigs: viii-ix-xi-xii.1 ♭ / iv.14 ♯ / vi.22 ♭ [whole folio er]
102. sigs: ii-iii-v-viii-ix-xi.1 ♭ / iv.1 ♯ / v.5 b♯ ; 15 ♭ / vi.9 ♭ / vii.9 ♯ ; 27 f / viii.5 c♯ ; 6 ♭ / x (original version.10 ♯ er ; 12 f er) ; 20 ♯ ; 22 ♯ / xii.4 ♭ ; 7 ♭ [whole folio er]
102 v.i.6 g♯ ; 7 g ; 9 ♯ / iii.5 ♭ / vii.2 ♯ / ix.15 ♯
103. i.7 g♯ / iv.15 ♯ / ix.17 ♭ ; 20 b♯ / x.2 ♯ ; 14 ♯
103v. iv.2 ♯
104. i.18 ♯ / iv.7 c♯ / viii.18 ♭ / ix. 4 ♭ ; 9 e♭ / xii.1 ♭ ; 2 e♭ ; 5 a♭ ; 14* a♯
104v. ii.10 ♯ / iv.6 c♯ ; 24 ♯ / v.14 ♯
105. i.15 g♯ ; 16 c♯ / iv.33 ♯ / vi.2 ♭
105v. i.1 ♯ ; 3 f / iii.15 ♭ / iv.5 ♯ / ix.19 ♭ / xi.15 ♭
106. ii.8 ♭ / iii.10 ♭ / v.2 ♭ ; 10 b♯ / vi.1 ♭ / vii.10 ♯ / xii.17 ♭
106v. i.1 ♯ / iv.2 ♯ / v.1 ♯ er / vii.7 ♯ viii.7 ♯ / xi.1 ♭
107. sigs: i to x.1 ♭,e♭,♭ / iii.8 ♯ / iv.9 b♯ ; 12 e♯ / vii.14* e♯ / ix.17 e♯
107v. sigs: ix to xii.1 ♭ / viii.19 ♭
108. i.7 ♯ / iii.18 ♯ / vii.11 ♭
109v. ii.20 ♯ / iv.31 ♭ / vi.11 ♯ ; 15 f ; 17 ♭
110. sigs: i-ii-iv to x.1 ♭ / ii.5 b♯
110v. i.2 ♭ / ii.6 ♭ / iii.30 ♭ / iv.5 ♭ / v.5 ♭ / vi.1 ♭ ; 32 ♭ / vii.3 ♭ / viii.1 ♭ ; 6 b♯
111. sigs: i to ix.1 ♭ / viii.2 b♯
111v. v.28 ♯
112. i.2 ♯ / iv.3 ♯ / vii.14 ♯ / ix.27 c♯
112v. v.18 ♭

BIBLIOGRAPHY

Not all of the works listed relate to the period 1350-1450: I have attempted to include all the major studies of musica ficta.

Allaire, G.: "The Theory of the Hexachords and Solmization and the Model System", *Musicological Studies and Documents* 24, American Institute of Musicology, Rome, 1971.

Apel, W.: "Accidentien und Tonalität in den Musikdenkmälern des 15. und 16. Jahrhunderts", Berlin 1936.

— "The Notation of Polyphonic Music, 900-1600", 5th ed., Cambridge, Massachusetts, 1953, *passim*.

— "The Partial Signatures in the Sources up to 1450", in *Acta Musicologica* X, 1938, pp.1-13.

— "A Postcript to *The Partial Signatures in the Sources up to 1450*", in *Acta Musicologica* XI, 1939, pp.40-42.

Bent, Margaret: "The Old Hall Manuscript: a Paleographical Study", dissertation, Cambridge 1968, *passim*. The Appendix entitled *Musica Ficta*, pp.389-429, is the most relevant section and is to be published separately, with revisions, under the title "Musica Recta, Musica Ficta and the Old Hall Manuscript".

Clercx, Suzanne: "Johannes Ciconia. Un musicien liégeois et son temps", 7 vols., Brussels 1960; uol. I, pp. 101-106, *passim*.

— "Les Accidents Sous-entendus et la Transcription en Notation Moderne", in *Les Colloques de Wégimont* II, 1955, pp. 167-195.

Coussemaker, E. de: "Scriptorum de Musica Medii Aevi", 4 vols., Paris 1864-1876; photographic reprint published Hildesheim 1963.

Ficker, Rudolf: "Beiträge zur Chromatik des 14. bis 16. Jahrhunderts", in *Studien zur Musikwissenschaft* II, 1914, pp. 5-33.

Hibberd, L.: "*Musica Ficta* and Instrumental Music c.1250-1350", in *Musical Quarterly* XXVIII, 1942, pp.216-226.

Hoppin, R. H.: "Conflicting Signatures Reviewed", in *Journal of the American Musicological Society* IX, 1956, pp.97-117.

— "Partial Signatures and Musica Ficta in some Early Fifteenth Century Sources", in *Journal of the American Musicological Society* VI, 1953, pp.197-215.

Hughes, Andrew: "The Old Hall Manuscript: a Re-appraisal", in *Musica Disciplina* XXI, 1957, pp.97-147.

— "Some Notes on the Early Fifteenth-Century Contratenor", in *Music & Letters* L, 1969, pp.376-387.

— "Ugolino: the Monochord and Musica Ficta", in *Musica Disciplina* XXIII, 1969, pp.21-39.

Jacobs, C.: "Spanish Renaissance Discussion of Musica Ficta", in *Proceedings of the American Philosophical Society*, vol. 112, 1968, pp.277-298.

Johnson, Martha: "A Study of Conflicting Key-Signatures in Francesco Landini's Music", in *Hamline Studies in Musicology*, ed. E. Krenek,

vol. 2, Minneapolis 1947.
Kottick, E. L.: "Flats, Modality and Musica Ficta in some Early Renaissance Chansons", in *Journal of Music Theory* XII, 1968, pp.264-280.
Levitan, Joseph: "Adrian Willaert's famous duo...", Amsterdam 1939 (reprint from *Tijdschrift der Vereeniging voor Muziekgeschiedenis* XV, 3e stuk, 1938; 4e stuk, 1939.)
Levy, K. J.: "Costeley's Chromatic Chanson", in *Annales Musicologiques* III, 1955, pp.213-263.
Lockwood, L.: "A Sample Problem of *Musica Ficta*...", in *Studies in Music History; Essays for Oliver Strunk*, ed. H. Powers, Princeton 1968, pp.161-182.
Lowinsky, E. E. L.: "Conflicting Views on Conflicting Signatures", in *Journal of the American Musicological Society* VII, 1954, pp.181-204.
— "Echoes of Adrian Willaert's Chromatic Duo...", in *Studies in Music History; Essays for Oliver Strunk*, ed. H. Powers, Princeton 1968, pp.183-238.
— Foreword to "Musica Nova", ed. H. C. Slim, Chicago & London 1964, pp.v-xxi.
— "The Function of Conflicting Signatures in Early Polyphonic Music", in *Musical Quarterly* XXXI, 1945, pp.227-260.
— "The Goddess Fortuna in Music", in *Musical Quarterly* XXIX, 1943, pp.45-77.
— "Matthaeus Greiter's *Fortuna*: an Experiment in Chromaticism...", in *Musical Quarterly* XLII, 1956, pp.500-519, continued in XLIII, 1957, pp.68-85.
— ed., "The Medici Codex"; first vol., *Historical Introduction and Commentary*, Chicago & London 1968, *passim*.
— "Secret Chromatic Art in the Netherlands Motet", transl. C. Buchman, New York 1946. Reviewed by Willi Apel in *Musical Quarterly* XXXII, 1946, pp.471-476.
Massera, Giuseppe: "Musica inspettiva e accordatura strumentale", in *Quadrivium* VI, 1964, pp. 85-105.
The Old Hall Manuscript, new edition, ed. Andrew Hughes and Margaret Bent, *Corpus Mensurabilis Musicae* 46, 3 vols., American Institute of Musicology, Rome 1969-1970.
Reaney, Gilbert: "Musica Ficta in the Works of Guillaume de Machaut", in *Les Colloques de Wégimont* II, 1955, pp.196-213.
Reaney, Gilbert: "The Ballades, Rondeaux and Virelais of Guillaume de Machaut...", in *Acta Musicologica* XXVII, 1955, pp.40-58.
— "Accidentals in Early Fifteenth Century Music", in *Renaissance-Muziek 1400-1600, Donum Natalicum René Bernard Lenaerts*, Louvain 1969, pp. 223-231.
Schrade, L.: "A Secret Chromatic Art", in *Musica Disciplina* I, 1946, pp.159-167.
Seay, A.: "The 15th-Century *Coniuncta*, a Preliminary Study", in *Aspects of Medieval and Renaissance Music, a Birthday Offering to Gustave*

Reese, ed. Jan LaRue, New York 1966, pp.723-737.
— ed., *Ugolini urbevetani declaratio musice discipline*, in *Corpus Scriptorum de Musica* 7, 3 vols., American Institute of Musicology, Rome 1959-1962.
Vogel, Martin: "Musica falsa und falso bordone", in *Festschrift für Walther Wiora*, ed. Ludwig Finscher & Christoph-Hellmut Mahling, Kassel 1967, pp. 170-176.

INDEX

References are to section numbers, printed bold at the beginning of paragraphs of the text: within sections 11, 12, & 13, small figures denote sentence numbers.

Multiple appearences of a term in one section are not recorded.

Figures printed bold in the Index refer to extended discussions.

Padua, Bibl. Univ. Ms 1225, fol. 2